MW00619510

Mysteries and Miracles of Texas

By Jack Kutz

Rhombus Publishing Company

Cover design and illustrations
by Mary Robert

Rhombus Publishing Company, Inc.
P.O. Box 806, Corrales, New Mexico 87048

Contents

Foreword

In Texas just about anything is possible and almost nothing is unbelievable. Here, in a state so vast that it boggles the mind with its sheer immensity, anything that can be imagined can become a reality.

Texas is a land where an oak tree can live for 2,000 years and a president can die in a split second; a land where a single acre in downtown Kilgore produced 2.5 million barrels of oil and the world's tallest windmill once rose to the skyscraper height of 132 feet above the XIT Ranch. Texas is a place where a lowly yucca can grow to be 20 feet tall, a catfish can weight 99 pounds and a hailstone can be as big as a softball.

Texas constantly goes from one extreme to another. A year of bone-dry drought may be followed by 109 inches of rain the next year. In winter, a sudden blue norther can drop the temperature to 25 below zero while a summer heat wave can send the mercury soaring to nearly 120 degrees. Just about everything in Texas is extraordinary —its size, its weather, its heroic history and its people's pride. The Lone Star State is like a tall tale come to life. But there is even more to Texas than boldness and bigness. Texas is also a land of mysteries and miracles.

If the state's natural wonders seem almost beyond belief, its supernatural phenomena are indeed totally incomprehensible. Texas' nights are filled with dreadful ghosts, powerful witches and frightful creatures that sail ominously across the darkened skies.

Many of Texas' mysteries are not supernatural, but they are still so strange that they defy all scientific explanation. Astonishing nocturnal lights repeatedly come out of nowhere; eerie sounds echo through the desert wastelands and stones bearing enigmatic messages have been found in the most unlikely places. Of course, it is not surprising that some of the nation's most spectacular UFO sightings and encounters have occurred in the sky and on the ground in Texas.

A number of Texas' most fascinating mysteries are the true-life tales about star-crossed people who were led by destiny to the wrong places at the wrong times to meet startling, unexplainable fates.

This book is a modest but carefully detailed attempt to gather as many of these near-forgotten mysteries as possible into a single volume, to preserve them before they fade away. From the start, I realized writing this book would be a challenging endeavor. Texas is so darn big, I thought. I'll never discover all her mysteries. And perhaps I didn't. Nonetheless, here in these 14 chapters are dozens of strange stories. Though some may be difficult to believe, they can't be dismissed.

My travels around Texas in search of these mysteries took me to many intriguing places I might never have visited and which resulted in some enthralling experiences. I spent a delightful evening sharing binoculars with the spellbound spook light watchers outside Marfa... roamed the whispering dunes of the Monahans Sandhills... hiked the haunted trails of Big Bend. On one unforgettable occasion, my wife, La Donna, and I weathered out a Padre Island storm nearly as ferocious as the one endured by the famous treasure hunters of 1967.

Whenever possible I have included specific directions for visiting these strange and magical places so you, the reader, can also experience them.

The mysteries and miracles of Texas come in both large and small sizes. Once, in 1897 in the little town of Eastland during construction of the local courthouse, a live horned toad was sealed in a cornerstone. In 1928 the courthouse was torn down; the cornerstone was broken open and the toad was found alive. It had survived without air, food or water and had not seen the light of day for 31 years.

Perhaps this book will free other mysteries from the darkness where they have been waiting to be rediscovered just as "Old Rip" the horned toad was so many years ago.

1

The Spook Lights of Marfa

Night has come once again to West Texas. Near Alpine, the Chinati and the Cienaga Mountains have all but disappeared into the darkness beyond the lonely two-lane blacktop that stretches from east to west across Brewster and Presidio Counties.

The hot afternoon wind has gentled into a cool breeze, and the empty landscape is quiet except for an occasional car rushing by on the highway, or a coyote calling faintly from the wasteland. More than 20 people

1

are gathered around the cars and recreational vehicles they have parked near a bronze plaque on the edge of the highway. They, too, are quiet as they stare into the night. Some are sharing binoculars while others stand atop concrete picnic tables or on the large boulders that line the roadside pull-off. All are alert, expectant as they scan the sky.

Then someone shouts: "There's one! Straight ahead! Way over there!" "Ohs" and "ahhs" go up, and a few people laugh with delight. A bright, white light has appeared in the distance.

The light is a long way away; its size cannot be determined, but it is much bigger than a star. It is stationary and constant. "There's another," a man with binoculars calls out. "Just to the left of the first one."

"Ranch lights?" a skeptic asks.

"Not this one," the sighter asserts. "It's definitely above the horizon; it's higher than the skyline."

Now several people are pointing to the southwest, toward the Chinati where two more pinpoints of light are now shining. "Could they be car lights?" one observer asks. "Maybe it's a couple of cars sitting on a mountain road with their lights on." As he speaks, both lights move simultaneously and horizontally to the right. Then they fade out only to reappear in their original positions a few minutes later.

The awed spectators continue their roadside vigil for a couple of hours. Then all but the most enthralled viewers return to their vehicles and head back for town. They drive away feeling rewarded and satisfied though a little bewildered since they have seen the fabled Spook Lights of Marfa with their own eyes.

For at least 150 years, people living in or passing through the rough, raw country north of Big Bend have been startled, mystified and sometimes frightened by the unexplainable aerial lights that glow almost nightly in the darkness beyond the small, rustic towns and the outskirts of the widely scattered ranches.

The lights nearly always show as round, brilliant globes but they behave in a variety of ways. They may hang motionless for hours or unexpectedly shoot up, zip sideway, or flip about as they fade and flicker. Single lights have been known to divide, spread apart into two circles and then join together again.

On a good night, these exotic phenomena put on a dazzling show. Their basic, near-incandescent white can change to yellow or soft green to blue or even red. Looking like multi-colored fireflies, they often perform a cosmic dance that seems to have been choreographed in the Spirit World.

The first reports of strange lights in the Chinati Range came from members of a caravan on its way up from Ojinaga, Mexico, over Chinati Mountain in the early 1840s. Naturally, these passionately devout travelers believed the lights were signs from God, guiding them on their way.

In 1883 one of Big Bend's earliest settlers, Robert Ellison and his wife saw a distant light while driving a herd of cattle from Alpine to Marfa. Justifiably, it frightened them; they thought it might be an Apache campfire. The next day, when they reached Marfa and told everyone about their sighting, the local folks showed no surprise. "Yeah, there're lights out there all right," they acknowledged. "We've always seen 'em."

These early observations were easily explained by people who had never seen an electric light bulb or an automobile headlight. To them, the lights were obviously ghosts... probably Indians haunting the sites of their deaths, or perhaps, the restless souls of Spanish gold seekers.

The first serious attempt to study the ghost lights was made by Walter T. Harris around the turn of the century after the railroads had finally come to the Texas plains. Harris, a surveyor for the Southern Pacific, was utterly fascinated by the presence of unexplainable lights in the nearly uninhabited land. He and some of his fellow surveyors used a triangulation method to pinpoint the lights' locations, but they came to the completely erroneous conclusion that the lights were far beyond the Chinatis, somewhere down in Mexico.

Other attempts to identify the elusive lights' exact locations have also been unsuccessful. For a time, a lot of folks believed these glowing ghosts were standing guard at buried treasures. According to a popular legend that circulated through the area for many years, there is a red handprint high on a cliff somewhere in the Chinatis. If it can be re-discovered, and if one is willing to stand beneath it at night, a ghost light will rise up nearby revealing, but also protecting, a hidden treasure.

Even more creative explanations for the Marfa Lights became popular following the end of World War II. During the war, a small air base had been established near Marfa —a dusty, windswept outpost where pilots were trained for overseas duty. The stories told about the base after it closed would have made good plots for science fiction movies.

It was said that the Marfa Army Air Base's security forces were so concerned by the mysterious lights appearing almost nightly over restricted areas that they continuously patrolled the outer perimeters of the base after dark. Then one night, as a student pilot was coming in for a landing, several Marfa Lights lined up at ground level near a runway, luring the young aviator into a crash on a mountain side.

Immediately, two radio-equipped jeeps raced to the scene. The advance jeep radioed back to say they were approaching a row of hovering lights. Then, with a squawk, the transmission ended in mid-sentence. Suddenly the men in the second jeep saw a fiery explosion in the darkness. When they reached the first jeep, it was burning; there was no trace of the men and the spook lights had vanished.

An even more outlandish story made the rounds in the early 1950s. According to this grandiose conspiracy theory, Marfa Army Air Base was not really a training field for fledgling pilots: it was actually a cover-up for a top secret military research project. At the same time that some of the nation's most brilliant scientists were creating the atomic bomb at an even more remote site —Los Alamos, New Mexico— an equally prestigious group at Marfa was engaged in developing a laser fusion weapon, a "death ray," which was to be used to kill Adolph Hitler by zapping his underground bunker.

Since the technology was so new and risky, anything could go wrong. And, of course, it did, the story goes. When the scientists attempted to test their futuristic invention, it blew up like a warehouse full of fireworks. The explosion completely obliterated the research center and sent a barrage of laser beams flashing skyward to punch holes in outer space. In through these holes came the Marfa Lights, and out went the few surviving scientists. They are still out there, floating about in another dimension.

These were fun stories to tell to gullible tourists, but no help in explaining the true origins of the lights. In fact, it has always been easier to figure out what they are not than what they are. It has been easy to rule out ranchers' yard lights and car or train headlights. After all, everyone knows where the ranches are located, where the roads are, and what times the trains roll through. Near the Chinati Mountains there is a tall, red-lighted communications tower, but no one has ever been foolish enough to mistake it for anything other than what it is.

Over the years, many individuals in the Marfa-Alpine-Shafter area tried to solve the mystery, but not until 1975 was a coordinated effort made. Don Witt, then a physics teacher at Sul Ross State University in Alpine, organized a diverse group of local citizens into an investigative field team. Witt's team included members of the Sul Ross Society of Physics Students, some hikers from the Big Bend Outdoor Club, several owners of CB-equipped vehicles and a couple of pilots. The plan was to approach the spook lights from the air in small planes, from the roads in pickup trucks and on foot in the rougher terrain.

It was a great idea, but they found it exasperatingly difficult to maintain communications among all of these units to direct them all to the right locations at the right times. After spending a number of frustrating, chilly March nights in the flats and in the foothills, Witt's team had to admit they were unable to get close enough to the lights to learn what they were.

Still, many people who were not searching for the lights, nor even expecting to see them have had sudden, startling close-up encounters with these weird illuminations. Virtually every rancher living between Marfa and Alpine or Shafter and Presidio has at least one stunning spook light story to tell. Hallie Stillwell, who grew up on a ranch in the Dead Horse Mountains about 50 miles south of Marathon, saw the lights quite often during her childhood. She remembered them as bright, flickering and flame-like. "They would kind of grow dim," Stillwell recalled. "Then they'd come back again, brighter'n ever."

The lights usually seemed to be far away and therefore, non-threatening. It was not until Hallie Stillwell was a young woman that she saw the lights up close, and it was a frightening experience.

Hallie and her sister were driving home one night well after dark. When they pulled up to the ranch's closed entrance gate, they saw two red lights just above the ground on the other side of the gate. The lights looked very much like tail lights, but there was no vehicle there. Customarily, the person on the passenger's side will hop out to open a ranch gate, but Hallie's frightened sister refused to leave the car. Cautiously, Hallie stepped out on the driver's side, tip-toed forward with her eyes constantly on the lights to unlatch the gate. She swung it wide and dashed back to the car. With both hands tightly gripping the steering wheel, she held her breath as she drove past the ominous illuminations, and made it on to the safety of the ranch house.

Hallie Stillwell continued to witness distant aerial lights many times over the years, but this particular sighting was the one and only time she came face-to-face with whatever it is that haunts the West Texas night.

Sometimes people who happened to be out on the great, featureless flatlands between the Chinatis and the Cienagas have made some spectacular observations quite by chance. In 1985, Robert Black, a graduate student in geology at Sul Ross University, took a friend from Austin on a Saturday hike to the top of Goat Mountain on the western edge of the Cienagas. After Black parked his pickup on a country road several miles west of the peak, they set off on foot. They had gotten a late start and had under-estimated the distance they would have to walk, so it was late afternoon when they reached the summit. Black gathered some geologic samples. As the sun set, they hurriedly climbed down the mountain.

When the two men reached the flats, they began to jog as fast as they could fearing they would never find the truck if it got totally dark. But that is exactly what happened: the hapless pair couldn't find the truck, so they resigned themselves to wait out the night in the brushy plain.

"It's gonna be a long night," Black told his friend as they tried to get comfortable on the ground. "But maybe some of those ghost lights I've been telling you about will show up to help us pass the time."

Sure enough, shortly before midnight, a large, white light appeared above the creosote bushes.

Black described it as long and horizontal, very bright and very close. Throughout the night, dozens of lights appeared and disappeared. They would pop straight up, vanish and re-appear to flit back and forth as they changed colors —from cold, bluish-white to warm, yellow-orange. When dawn finally came, the awestruck hikers headed off toward the now-visible truck scarcely able to believe they had actually attended a Marfa Spook Light dance.

Usually the people who see the lights at close range are in their cars at the time, traveling through the night at highway speeds. This can be very alarming, as Ophelia Ward, of Alpine, found out in 1973. She was driving by herself between Marfa and Alpine when she passed the Marfa Lights observation site. At that very moment, a bright, orange-red light flashed up and flew directly at her van. The glowing, spinning circle was about two and a half feet wide and moving very rapidly. The terrified woman pressed the accelerator to the floorboard, but the light continued to race alongside of her at fence-top level, about 20 feet from the road's southern shoulder. Although Ward pushed the speedometer up to 90, she could not lose the fiery globe until she neared the outskirts of Alpine. At last it vanished.

Ophelia Ward braked her van back down to a safe speed and cruised slowly but shakily beneath the more familiar street lights of Alpine.

Other times the Marfa Lights have actually come to the official observation site itself. Some viewers have reported seeing lights poised just beyond the fence, while others have watched spellbound as "little fireballs" rolled through the fence and bounced across the highway.

One night in 1986, a Fort Davis couple, Suzanne and Buck Parchman, were sitting in their car at the viewing site, peering south. Suddenly Suzanne screamed. Two glaring headlight-sized, white lights were swerving at them like a car completely out of control. The Parchmans braced for a collision, but the lights stopped at the window and "winked out."

Most direct contacts with Marfa Lights have been, and continue to be, on or near ground level. However, since the sky seems to be the lights' natural environment, it is not surprising that pilots have reported the lights higher up. For at least two generations, private pilots of West Texas have told incredible stories about the astonishing lights they have seen in the night sky, sometimes at a distance and sometimes uncomfortably close. Eddie Halsell's story is one of the more frightening.

Back in the 1960s, Halsell was a passenger in a small aircraft which was flying after dark toward the

Chinatis. As the plane neared the mountains, he and the pilot saw a far-away gleaming dot in the sky. Neither of them thought much about it at first; they had both seen Marfa Lights before. Then they realized this was no ordinary spook light. It was rapidly increasing in size and rushing straight at them, homing in on the plane like a heat-seeking missile.

In a brilliant, white flash, the ball of light engulfed the aircraft, blinding the shocked flyers. "It was bigger than the plane," Halsell said afterward. "We were inside the light. We couldn't see to fly."

The pilot banked the plane to the right, then to the left, trying desperately to escape the incandescent glare. Both men were on the verge of panic when, as quickly as it had come, the light was gone. The trembling pilot flew on over the Chinatis and made a safe landing in Presidio.

Just what are these mysterious lights? Are they a marvelous, unknown natural phenomenon, or are they something totally unnatural —something to be feared?

Jack Reed, of Shafter, is one person who definitely believes people should be afraid of them. Reed has been seeing the Marfa Lights since he was a little boy. He once awoke during the night to behold a six-foot tall, yellow light hovering in front of his house. He also claims the lights have stopped the engine of his car on several occasions.

Reed is sure the lights are manifestations of the Devil, that they come straight out of Hell through holes in the mountains. No one, he stresses, should ever willingly go near one.

Others disagree. Some observers, such as former Alpine resident Robin Campbell, find the experience a mystic one. She claims that one came within 50 yards of her. "When I saw that ball of light, it created in me a feeling of happiness and joy and magic," Campbell said.

Once, on a winter night in 1975, a retired Alpine businessman, Verne Campbell, saw one of the lights while it was snowing. It was a nearly indescribably beautiful sight, he said; the sparkling snowflakes fell as though the softly shimmering light was shedding moonbeams.

Still, whether the lights are natural and benign or unnatural and ominous, there has to be an explanation for them. As Alpine bookstore owner Judith Brueske wrote in her book, **The Marfa Lights**: "One would think that a mystery of such long standing would have been solved by now, but it hasn't. While most proposed explanations are persuasive to some extent, no one of them seems to fit all the cases reported."

Some have suggested that luminous gases may be the source of the lights. But so-called swamp gas, or "will-o-the wisps," appear almost exclusively in wet, marshy terrain, certainly not in dry, semi-desert country. It is natural gas perhaps? Could the area's natural gas deposits be leaking from the ground to be ignited by spontaneous combustion or static electricity?

Or, are the lights phosphorescent glows from mineral deposits in and near the mountains? This would seem to be only a remote possibility since phosphorescence is always faint and does not travel around.

To many people, ball lightning is an attractive explanation. The problem with this theory is that ball lightning itself is an inexplicable phenomenon. These strange, unearthly-looking balls are indisputably real, for they have been seen and photographed many times. They cannot be dismissed, but they cannot be explained.

Ball lightning can and does pop up suddenly and unexpectedly in many shapes and sizes. It can be as big as a house or as tiny as a flashlight bulb. Usually it is white or yellow, but it can just as easily be blue, violet or red. These cold flames move swiftly in startling ways, flashing up and down, flying toward observers or simply gliding slowly past them before vanishing in the blink of an eye.

So far scientists have only speculated about the causes of these glowing spheres. They have considered such possibilities as reactions created by electromagnetic forces, anti-matter meteorites, violent chemical reactions in the atmosphere, and even intense cosmic radiation. But nothing has been proven to anyone's complete satisfaction.

Interestingly, even if the true nature of ball lightning is conclusively determined someday, it will not solve the mystery of the Marfa Lights which have repeatedly demonstrated they can do things ball lightning cannot. A burst of ball lightning lasts no longer than 10 to 15 seconds; a Marfa Light can hang in the air for hours. When ball lightning abruptly disappears, it is invariably accompanied by a thunderous, explosive noise, whereas the Marfa Lights are always eerily silent.

Another intriguing theoretical explanation is that the mystery lights may be mirages. Like bank-shots in a pool game, refracted lights can sometimes bounce from their origin to someplace quite distant. Air currents of differing temperatures and densities may form reflective surfaces capable of throwing lights the way a ventriloquist might throw a voice.

If so, it is conceivable that a Marfa Light observer may be seeing the distorted refraction of a light that is far away, below the horizon or behind a mountain.

Admittedly, this type of phenomenon would not explain all the Marfa Light sightings, but probably no single explanation can. It seems unlikely that lights that can dance, fly, roll on the ground and chase cars will ever be placed in one specific category.

Over the years, the Marfa Lights have gotten the attention of scientists from around the world. Yoshi Ohtsuki, head of the Department of Physics at Tokyo's Waseda University, has a life-long interest in ball lightning and similar phenomena. His fascination began when, at the age of 13, he watched a great, white ball of light drift over a forest in northern Japan.

In 1989, Ohtsuki accompanied a Japanese television crew to Marfa to document the famous lights on film. The crew's nightly vigilance was rewarded by the capture of a very unusual light on the video tape. It was long and thin like a piece of string which shortened very quickly into a ball. Ohtsuki suspected, but was far from certain, that the illumination might be an electrostatic phenomenon caused by changes in daytime and nighttime temperatures and humidity.

Three years later, Ohtsuki returned to Marfa, this time with a very impressive international scientific team. State-of-the-art atmospheric equipment, cameras with telephoto lenses, and all manner of recording devices were flown in and set up at a base camp not far from the official viewing site. Ohtsuki, acknowledging there might be something spiritual about the lights, had brought along a Buddhist priest.

Each evening at sundown, the holy man performed a ritual to summon up the lights. During the first two nights, nothing happened. "We watched and watched," Ohtsuki said. "But there wasn't anything to witness."

Then, on the third night after the priest finished

chanting, a very bright light appeared on the horizon.

Through the camera crew's telephoto lenses, it was an awesome sight. The light flickered and flashed in different colors. It repeatedly divided into two identical parts and reunited again. However, this spectacular performance was not the only amazing aspect that Ohtsuki's team recorded that warm September evening in 1989.

Just before the light made its debut, Edson Hendricks, a San Diego expert in the science of spherics, was using a sophisticated sound detection device to listen to the atmosphere. Suddenly he began hearing a long, descending pitch signal; moments later, the light came on. During the nights that followed, Hendricks heard and recorded the faint, whistle-like sound that seemed to preceed the appearance of a Marfa Light on many occasions.

Yoshi Ohtsuki's team gathered an impressive amount of data, but when he left Texas that fall he had to admit he could reach no conclusions about the true nature of the lights.

Edson Hendricks was especially fascinated by some very curious images that appeared on several photographs he shot while at the base camp. Using infrared film, Hendricks had photographed the sky at times when no aerial lights were visible. Yet after the film was developed, strange spots could be seen in the photos. Were these infrared flashes or light, or just some imperfection in the film quality?

Hendricks and independent researcher Robert Creasey of Palo Alto, California, returned to Marfa in the spring of 1993. Over a week's time they took infrared pictures of the black Texas sky. When developed, the photos showed the same anomalous spots. Either Hendricks had used dozens of rolls of bad film two years in a row, or there is something going on out there in the night that is invisible to the unaided human eye.

Each time something new is discovered about the Marfa Lights, the mystery seems only to deepen. Puzzles within puzzles continue to merge; more questions demand answers. No doubt the day will come when this tantalizing mystery will at last be solved. But until that day arrives, expectant skywatchers will keep on gathering nightly on the edge of the lonely Texas highway that passes through this bleak but enchanted landscape, each hoping to be able to say the next morning: "Yes, I saw them. I saw the Marfa Lights."

How to Visit the Marfa Lights

From Marfa, drive east on Highway 67-90. Watch for a "Historical Marker- 1 Mile" sign approximately eight miles from town. Proceed on to the marker which is an easily overlooked bronze plaque set on the south side of the edge of the highway. Park in the semi-circular, graveled pull-off designated as the official Marfa Lights observation site.

When one faces south, the Chinati Mountains are to the right, and the Cienagas are to the left. A pair of binoculars greatly enhances the fine art of spook light watching.

Bibliography - Chapter 1

Brueske, Judith M. **The Marfa Lights.** Alpine, Texas. Ocotillo Enterprises. 1988. Revised 1989.

Brueske, Judith M. **The Desert Candle.** Alpine, Texas. Ocotillo Enterprises. May-June, 1993.

Corliss, William R. **Handbook of Unusual Natural**

Phenomena. New York. Arlington House, Inc. 1977.

Miles, Elton. **Marfa Lights.** Alpine, Texas. Sul Ross State University. 1990.

Stewart, Richard. *Houston Chronicle.* March 26, 1989.

Transcript of *Sightings.* Fox Television. March 26, 1993.

2
The Mysterious Spider Rock

"Cover your eyes, Lucretia," John Sems said. "We're almost there." The statuesque, long-haired woman sitting beside him on the wagon seat pressed her hands over her face, concealing both her eyes and her smile.

The covered wagon creaked forward and came to a stop on the edge of a small rise in the heart of the wild, rough landscape. "You can take a look now," John said. "And everything you can see belongs to us. I know it's a pretty rough piece of land, but it's all ours, Lucretia. I hope you're not disappointed."

Lucretia Sems lowered her fingers and gazed across the harsh, hot slope spreading out before her. It was, indeed, a "rough piece of land," thick with underbrush and studded with scrub oaks and prickly pear. Lucretia's dark eyes squinted against the glare, her smile widened. "I love it already," she beamed.

She lifted her long skirt above her ankles,

stepped down from the wagon and stood for the first time on the sandy soil upon which she and her husband would spend the rest of their lives. Here, in Callahan County on the edge of the wind-swept western plains, they would build their home, clear their fields and raise seven daughters and a son.

And here, too, they would learn that they had settled on one of the most mysterious places in all of Texas.

Lucretia Sems did sincerely love the stark sprawl of coarse land where she and John carved out their ranch. During the first few years, the Sems had little time for anything other than work. But whenever possible, Lucretia explored the land acre by acre until one day, she found something rather strange.

In the southernmost 80 acres, which they had never even attempted to develop, she came upon a pile of stones with a tall rock set up beside them like a tombstone. Nearby were three oak trees which apparently had been braided together when they were saplings. They were now large trees, still entwined.

That evening, Lucretia told John about her discovery. He was as puzzled as she. "Maybe it's an Indian grave," he ventured. "No one else ever lived on this land." Lucretia accepted this explanation until in 1908, nine years after the Sems had moved onto the property, a stranger rode up to their cabin.

He was a heavy-set man who appeared to be in his early seventies; his hair and beard were long and white. He introduced himself as Dave Arnold and asked to stay the night. The Sems never turned any travelers away from their door, so they welcomed him in.

At supper, Arnold told the Sems about himself and his quest. Framed in chiaro scuro by the lantern on the table, the pale-eyed old man said he had lived for several years in Mexico where he learned how to read old Spanish markings chiseled on rocks... markings which, if one knew how to interpret them, could lead to hidden treasures. Arnold said he was currently following a "line" of such markings from Mexico north up through Texas. Each marker gave the distance to the next and offered a clue as to where it would be found. The trail of markers had led him to the Sems' ranch.

"I feel my search has nearly ended," Arnold said. "Now I must find three trees braided together."

Lucretia Sems was speechless for a second. "There are three braided trees here on our land," she gasped.

Dave Arnold could scarcely contain his excitement. "Then it is here!" he exclaimed. "Mr. and Mrs. Sems, there is a treasure buried somewhere on your ranch! I must see those trees first thing in the morning."

When daylight came, Arnold and the Sems trooped off to look at the twisted oaks. "No doubt about it," Arnold said when he saw them. "This is the place, all right. Now the first thing we must do is locate the 'plat rock.' It will be beneath the ground, of course, so it will take some digging. But once we find it, its markings will tell us exactly where the treasure is."

Arnold sat down on the tombstone-shaped rock in front of the trees and thought for a minute. "Mister Sems," he said at last. "I have a proposition to make to you. I realize this is your land and any treasure that is buried on it is rightfully yours. However, when we find that rock, I will be the only one of us able to read it. I suggest we become partners and share whatever we find. I'm sure there is enough wealth under this land to make us both very happy. Let's go 50-50. How does that sound?"

"Sounds fair to me," John Sems said. "Let's go

get some shovels." Through the rest of the day, John and Dave spaded up soil that had lain undisturbed for at least a century. They dug beneath the roots of the woven trees and under the pile of rocks. They found nothing.

Day after day, the two men dug further out in each direction around the braided oaks, but still they found nothing. Sems was growing discouraged and a bit skeptical. "Dave," he said, "I can't neglect my fields much longer. We have plantin' to do, and Lucretia can't do it all by herself."

"I understand," Arnold replied. "Tend to your fields and cattle, John. I'll continue to search."

For an old man, Arnold labored well. From their fields, John and Lucretia could see him in the distance steadily tossing shovelfuls of dirt throughout the day. Then just at dusk one day, he trudged up to the cabin with a triumphant grin on his tired face.

"I found it," he said as he plunked down on the porch steps. "The plat rock. The reason we didn't find it earlier was that it is embedded in the roots of an oak that has grown up around it. Tomorrow we can go back down there with an axe and free that stone. Oh, I can hardly wait to learn what it has to tell us!"

The sun had barely cleared the horizon when the two eager men began hacking away at the tangle of roots protectively clutching an irregularly shaped, coarsely-textured grey rock. Within an hour they were able to slide it out into the open.

Arnold tapped it with his knuckle. "The plat rock has been preserved in pulverized, oiled charcoal," he explained. "We can chisel it off, but we must be very careful. We don't want to damage the stone itself."

Cautiously he crumbled the charcoal with the head of an axe and brushed it away. In the center of this crust, he uncovered a piece of white sandstone.

The stone was circular, about three feet in circumference, and barely an inch thick. It had been delicately carved with a large circle in the center surrounded by two thinner circles through which four straight, intersecting lines had been etched.

"It looks like a spider web," Sems said.

"It does indeed," Arnold agreed. "Let's turn our spider rock over and see what the other side looks like. Easy now....Oh, my! Look at that, John. Whoever carved this stone was quite an artisan, wouldn't you say?"

The underside of the small slab of sandstone bore an intricately sketched maze of circles and lines, symbols and numbers. Each marking had been filled with molten copper, making the stone a very beautiful object.

"Can you make any sense out of it?" Sems asked.

"Oh yes, but it will take a bit of study," Arnold replied as he took his glasses out of his vest pocket. "The first thing we can be sure of is that, since this side of the stone was facing down, its markings refer to underground workings. That tiny dot in the center represents the plat rock itself, so that's where we're standing now."

His eyes scanned the stone a moment. "Here's an 'N.' Obviously that means 'north.' The straight lines going out in all directions will lead us to other clues. The double lines may well indicate the existence of tunnels below our feet. But... here's something disturbing. See those wavy lines at the end of each 'tunnel line?' Lines like that always symbolize water. It's quite probable the tunnels were slanted down until they hit underground water, so our treasure may be submerged.

"What is the water level on your property, John?"

Sems spread his hands. "I have no idea. We've never been able to afford to drill a well. We have a stock pond that catches rainwater, but we have to haul our drinkin' water from the creek two miles away."

Dave Arnold pointed a finger at the numerals embossed alongside each of the four water markings. "Twenty-nine," he said. "I'd wager that if you ever do put down a well, you'll hit water at 29 feet.

"Now," he continued. "Look at this... each of these 'tunnel lines' has a number beside it, like this one, for example: 'LXXX.' That would be 80 *varas* which is a little over 200 feet. In front of that number there's a sort of upside-down teardrop symbol. From that juncture, the tunnel veers off at a sharp angle, so the symbol marks that turning point. Let's pace it out and see what we can find."

With the stone held reverently in his hands, Arnold strode in measured steps away from the center of the Spider Rock maze. After counting 80 paces, he stopped and looked around. "Sure enough," he said. "There it is, chiseled on a rock. Only it's not a teardrop; it's an eye. That means we must look in exactly that direction."

Arnold began pacing off the land again with the fascinated John Sems following. Throughout the day they found more markings... circles, half-circles, a horizontal arrow, but nothing indicating where to dig.

That night Arnold painstakingly made a paper copy of the Spider Rock. "We'll take this with us tomorrow and leave the stone here in the house so we don't risk breaking it," he explained. "And we'll take along some shovels. It's possible we may find additional clues underneath the markings."

The two men returned to the "eye rock" the next

THE SPIDER ROCK. Each new clue that it yielded only deepened its mystery.

morning to begin digging below it. At a depth of three feet, they unearthed a curious object. Dave Arnold lifted it and shook his head in bewilderment. "It's a stone duck," he said. "Someone went to a lot of trouble to carve this, but what on earth could it mean? Well, let's move on."

Beneath the next marked rock, the perspiring pair shoveled up a thin strip of copper shaped like a number "1." At the third marker, a small copper disk emerged. Arnold was growing more and more perplexed until, under a rock bearing a circle with dots pecked in the center, he dug up a copper dagger six inches long.

"Now we're on to something!" he said excitedly. "This knife was pointing down. That clearly means 'go deeper.' Are you ready for some more digging, John?"

John Sems answered by pushing his shovel into the sandy soil.

The two men dug throughout the rest of the day and returned to dig again in the morning. Soon word got out around Callahan County that a treasure hunt was in progress on the Sems Ranch. Several men from neighboring farms and ranches showed up to volunteer their help, so the hole rapidly grew deeper as the mounds of dirt above it rose higher.

Arnold supervised additional digging under the other markers. The earth yielded a number of odd relics: a lead arrow, a small star and rocks with strange symbols carved on them.

Back at the main hole, the diggers had reached a layer of yellow clay which looked unnatural. It appeared to have once been wet and to have been slicked down by hand in the same manner that adobe mud is applied to walls. Arnold urged his crew to carefully remove the soil around this flat section of clay.

When they had done so, they found an arched doorway filled with pure, white sand.

Workers gently sifted out the sand and made a very macabre discovery. On the floor of the chapel-like archway, four decayed skeletons lay side by side, facing up. The ground below the bones had never been disturbed, so they figured there was no reason to dig deeper.

Although the tomb fascinated the men who had unearthed it, Arnold was deeply disappointed. He had followed the Spider Rock's every clue and had found nothing but a pile of bones. He was at a total loss as to where to dig next until Lucretia made a suggestion. She said she had heard that there was a clairvoyant woman, a Mrs. Matlock, living in Abilene. She was supposed to be able to go into trances and find lost objects. Lucretia thought perhaps Mrs. Matlock could locate the treasure.

The woman did agree to try. She visited the ranch a few days later and went into several trances during which she gave directions to a variety of places. This resulted in a hodge-podge of renewed digging but turned up no treasure or additional artifacts.

After Matlock left, Arnold grew completely disheartened. He stood with the Sems on the edge of their pock-marked piece of land and declared, "This is a mystery beyond my ability to solve. Somewhere, buried in that ground out there, is an immense fortune, but I'm afraid we are not the ones destined to find it. I'm calling it quits, my friends. I'm going back to the house to start packing my things."

"Me and Lucretia will be goin' back to the fields," said John. "See you at supper, Dave."

At sundown, the weary Sems returned to their home and found that Dave Arnold was gone. And so was the Spider Rock. John Sems felt betrayed. "He didn't have to steal it," he told Lucretia. "I'd have given it to him if he'd asked."

The Sems never knew why Arnold took the stone since the old man was never seen again in that part of Texas. Perhaps he planned to sell it, or maybe he just couldn't bear to part with it. Arnold had left the paper copy behind so the Sems rolled it up, tucked it away and went back to their hard-scrabble lives as Texas ranchers.

A few years later, an Abilene businessman, Gurney Ward, decided to take up the search where Arnold left off. Ward believed the first attempt failed because it had been conducted on too small a scale; he proposed to launch his search in a big way.

Gurney Ward signed a contract with John Sems giving him a sizeable percentage of whatever was found. He then formed a company and sold shares in the treasure to finance the work. A large crew of pick-and-shovel men were hired. Tents for them were set up near the digging site.

Ward planned to excavate each of the "tunnels" shown on the copy. When Sems warned him about the possibility of hitting water at 29 feet, Ward decided to dig to nearly that level and extend his trenches above the water. After several months of work, Ward's laborers dug out all of the "tunnel lines." The change in the texture of the earth at the depth of 22 feet on down to 27 feet convinced Ward there had once actually been tunnels here. But why? There was nothing in them now.

The businessman realized he would have to go below the groundwater level somehow. He ordered his men to dig into the aquifer which, as predicted, was struck at 29 feet. Ward installed a windmill to begin pumping out the water. It was an exercise in futility; the water level refused to drop.

By now Gurney Ward was running low on funds. His workers, now being paid with promises instead of cash, gradually all packed up and moved on. Ward abandoned his project and went back to face his disgruntled investors in Abilene. All John and Lucretia Sems got out of the project was a well, a windmill and a spiderweb network of collapsing sandy trenches.

But interest in the mystery would not fade away. In 1924, a leathery, old treasure hunter named Dock Henderson made up his mind to renew the search. He felt there was no point in further digging in the Spider Rock circle, so he began systematically exploring the land east of the Sems' ranch.

It didn't take Dock long to find the rocky formation of an old Spanish mission which had once consisted of four small rooms. In the early 18th Century, the Spanish built several churches in the Texas wilderness in an unsuccessful attempt to bring the Hasinai and Caddoan Indian tribes into the embrace of Catholicism. Nearly all the missions failed; perhaps this had been one of them.

Henderson moved further east, carefully probing the dense hackberry thickets until, behind one of the bushes, he found an "eye rock" staring directly at the ruins of an old tumbled-down smelter. Around the smelter, Dock dug up a lot of copper and lead slag, but nothing of value.

Many marked rocks existed in the area, and Dock found them all one by one. Then late one Sunday afternoon, he came upon a marking that took his breath away. It was a depiction of a pot with legs; he was sure it indicated a pot of gold.

Dock Henderson was strictly a weekend treasure

hunter, so the week that followed must have been one of the longest of his life as he waited for Friday night. As soon as he got off work, he hurried back to the "pot rock" only to find that the property owner had hired a crew of Mexican laborers to grub out the mesquite in that section.

The workers had found the rock, rolled it away and dug up the pot. Henderson could still see its imprint in the soil. There was no way to know how much gold it contained but it must have been considerable for the laborers didn't even wait to collect their back wages before riding off to Mexico.

Henderson was angry but not entirely discouraged. He was sure there were more treasures out there waiting to be revealed.

By now Henderson had been joined by a fellow cedar brakes treasure hunter named Reid. Together they stepped off the distances from several numbered rocks. At one site, they spaded out an exquisite, silver statuette approximately seven inches tall. Less than a mile away, they uncovered another one.

For the most part, they found mere trinkets: silver arrows, a silver star and two silver crosses worn as collar pins. Then one weekend, the pair dug up a Spanish water *olla* filled with gold nuggets.

Henderson was jubilant, but when he got back to town Sunday night, he was absolutely furious. "That damned, dirty Reid!" he told his friends. "I turned my back on him for ten minutes and he threw everything we'd found into his Model T and took off for parts unknown. He stole all of it!"

Dock Henderson, like the others before him, decided he'd had enough; he had no desire to go on digging up trinkets.

In 1933, the last of the Spider Rock treasure

seekers arrived in the area. His name was Frank Olmstead, a married man from Lawton, Oklahoma. Olmstead had purchased a 133-acre tract of land not far from Henderson's digging. He felt sure that with a little perseverance he would find treasure on his own property.

He built a half-dugout into a rocky bluff and made walls of mud-mortared rock slabs. In one of the walls, he installed an old car windshield for a window. For a roof, he piled up a lattice-work of skinny logs and branches covered with brush. When Olmstead's wife realized he actually expected her to live in this pathetic hovel, she promptly divorced him in disgust and went back to Oklahoma.

Frank Olmstead didn't seem to mind. He was obviously born to be a hermit. He loved the wind-swept isolation that surrounded him with silence and hidden secrets.

Olmstead didn't need much money to support his spartan lifestyle. He picked cotton on neighboring farms and helped harvest crops of corn and black-eyed peas. In the latter case, he always asked to be paid with a portion of the crop. Consequently, Frank Olmstead never went hungry nor completely broke. Once a week he walked five miles to his mailbox to pick up the magazines and newspapers to which he subscribed. He lived a simple contented life. And he also dug for gold.

Olmstead explored his land thoroughly, looking for indentations in the soil or places where rocks appeared to have been moved around. When he found such a spot, he would put down a shaft, sometimes to a depth of 20 feet or more. He climbed into these shafts with a rope ladder, filled a bucket of dirt, climbed back up and pulled the bucket up on a rope. Over and over, he emptied the bucket, sifted and sent it back down.

For 15 years, until his death in 1943, Frank Olmstead kept up this relentless, tedious work. And he never found a damned thing.

Perhaps the Spider Rock area had yielded all the treasure, artifacts and curiosities it had to give. Even so, it remains a mysterious place. No one will ever know what kind of settlement once existed there.

One can only speculate as to why such an elaborate and extensive system of markings was created throughout the Spider Rock site and its outlying locations. Could it be the markers were meant to confuse rather than guide? Might they have been placed to lure searchers toward petty treasures and away from something of much greater importance?

Such conjecture leads nowhere, just as the Spider Rock's maze led to no major finds. But it does remain possible that something astounding may still be waiting undisturbed somewhere below the surface of this wide and desolate stretch of mysterious land.

Bibliography - Chapter 2

Mahan, William. **Early Spanish Treasure Signs and Symbols.** Garland, Texas. Little Treasures Publishing Company. 1964.

Sems, Verne. *True West.* Austin, Texas. Western Publications. July-August, 1966. December-January, 1971.

Wilson, Steve. *True West.* Austin, Texas. Western Publications. May-June, 1964. August, 1965.

3

THE GHOSTS OF TEXAS
ARE UPON YOU

They're everywhere.

Out on the wind swept plains, in the rolling hills of the east, and in the raw, jagged mountains of Big Bend, the ghosts of Texas are always present. They move fleetingly through the thickets, appear unexpectedly on the banks of rivers, and wait for travelers on dark, back-country roads. Texas is a *very* haunted place.

Due to the vastness and diversity of the state's terrain, there are haunted places of all possible kinds, and every imaginable type of phantom has, at one time or another, been sighted in Texas. Some of these ghosts are terrifying; some are harmless, and some are just pesky. Many are lost souls wandering eternally in search of things they left behind in their mortal lives, while other ghosts seem to have come back specifically to help the living.

Texas' most renown spirit is, of course, the famous ghost-witch *La Llorona*. This anguished, weeping phantom has been seen time and again in Texas, New Mexico and Old Mexico. She has, in fact, shown up in so many places over so many years that she cannot be dismissed as merely a spooky, folkloric legend.

La Llorona is said to be a woman who killed her children. Later, in remorse, she killed herself. Now she walks by night with her long, black hair flowing down over the shoulders of her full-length gown, forever wailing in her sorrow.

Though this ever-suffering apparition has been sighted and heard in many parts of Texas, one of the best places to catch a glimpse of her seems to be in and near Fort Stockton in Pecos County where *La Llorona* reportedly makes frequent appearances along the tree-lined waterway adjacent to Comanche Springs and in St. Joseph's Catholic Cemetery.

A Fort Stockton resident, Lee Harris, used to tell of the times when the local children would creep up at night to the edge of this bleak graveyard to watch for *La Llorona*. "They'd come runnin' back all wide-eyed and outta breath, swearin' they'd seen her walkin' through the crosses," Harris remembered. "Those kids were always so scared it was pretty hard not to believe 'em."

Other ghosts may have been mistaken for *La*

Llorona; they resembled her but do not behave at all like the more famous apparition. A good example is that reported by Lucy B. Dearen and her husband in the deep, piney woods of East Texas' Henderson County in 1915.

The Dearens were heading home late one night in a horse-drawn buggy along a meandering country road through the densely wooded Kickapoo Bottom. They rounded a curve in the road and were startled to see a beautiful, dark-haired woman in a long, white dress sitting on a fallen log. As the Dearens rode silently past her, the woman stared intently at them, but remained completely motionless and expressionless.

"That haint was so close I could've leaned out and touched her," Lucy Dearen told her neighbors the next day. "And the strangest thing of all was how our old horse acted. As y'all know, Old Bill is pretty skittish. Why, he'll shy and bounce if he sees a feather flutterin' on a weed, but he just walked on by. He never even seen her.

"After we was down the road aways, we both looked over our shoulders, and there wasn't nobody sittin' on that log. Henry said, 'I believe we have jest seen *La Llorona.*' But I said, 'No, I don't think so because *La Llorona* is always weepin' and wailin'. I believe what we seen must of been some other kind of haint.'"

The female phantoms of Texas have made similar appearances on the darkened backroads from the earliest days to the present time. Usually they are seen simply walking slowly through the night or standing silently in the moonlight. They are always scary to see but sometimes an encounter with one of these spirits can be a completely unnerving experience.

In the 1960s, a friend of Lee Harris was driving

by night on Highway 1035 between Imperial and Fort Stockton when his headlights illuminated the figure of a woman dressed in white standing by the road. As he drove past her, she flew swiftly toward the car and attached herself to the door simply by pressing her hands on it. As she peered in the window, the driver accelerated and swerved back and forth. But the ghost continued to cling to the car for nearly 10 miles before suddenly flying away.

This weird phenomenon re-occurred several times, always on the same stretch of road and only with the same car. Sometimes other people were in the car and they, too, saw the apparition.

According to Harris, the bedeviled driver was killed in a car wreck approximately one year after the ghost first appeared. Could it be the phantom knew this man was destined to die soon, and was trying to warn him? Or did she cause his death? Those questions Lee Harris and friends of the doomed man would ponder for the rest of their lives.

Encounters with roadside ghosts were even more frightening in the old days when people traveled in open buggies, without roll-up windows and locked doors. Around the turn of the century, Jack Boales, sheriff of Real County west of San Antonio, had a horrifying experience with a ghost. At the time he was courting a pretty, young woman who would later become his wife. One night after attending a social gathering up in the hills, the couple was returning to town on a deserted road through a dark valley. Suddenly the buggy came to an abrupt halt.

Boales, thinking he had hit a rock or a log, popped the reins, but the wheels would not turn. Both he and his future wife looked down to see what was blocking their buggy's progress. She began to scream hysterically. Entangled in the spokes of one of the front wheels was a thrashing, clawing, headless phantom.

Sheriff Boales lashed his horse frantically; the snorting animal pulled with all its might and the wheel spun at last, tossing the ghastly thing away. The buggy plunged ahead and Sheriff Boales drove at breakneck speed all the way back to town.

In the morning, the sheriff rounded up several men to go back with him to scene of the incident. Boales was not the least surprised when they found no trace of a headless body. He was sure that whatever it was blocked his wheel the previous night would not be the sort of thing that would be seen in broad daylight.

One of Texas' strangest ghost stories is The Wolf Girl of Devil's River. Her story is utterly bizarre from start to finish, for her earthly life was just as incredible as her spirit life.

The Wolf Girl was born in May of 1835. Her parents were John and Mollie Pertul Dent, a couple of would-be pioneers who were heading down the Devil's River Trail in hopes of settling in John Charles Beals' colony at Delores. The Dents were traveling alone, bravely but naively, through a very hostile landscape. They obviously did not know that the Beals colony had already failed (it had been abandoned for more than a year), nor that the fearsome Comanche Indians were raiding across the land.

The Dents' lonely journey along this near-empty and very dangerous stretch of trail was slow because Mollie was pregnant. Although John drove as carefully as possible, Mollie still winced at every jolt in the rutted road. Then one morning, she gave birth to a baby girl. The proud parents decided to stay in their makeshift camp for a few days so Mollie could rest. It was there that the Comanches found them.

The Dents had been dead for at least a week before their bodies were discovered by Mexican sheep-herders. The *pastores* also found a small baby blanket in a basket. Since the basket was empty and there were moccasin tracks and wolf pawprints all around the camp site, the shepherd concluded that the entire family had been slain by Indians and that, later, the baby's body had been eaten by wolves.

There the story rested for the next 14 years... just another all-too-common frontier tragedy... until 1849.

One summer night that year, a young Mexican boy was tending a flock of sheep near San Felipe Springs (as Del Rio was called in those days.) As the boy sat listening to the night, he heard the distant howls of a pack of wolves. Before long, the wolves came creeping out of the shadows on the edge of the pasture.

Bravely the young shepherd jumped up and ran toward them, shouting, throwing rocks and brandishing a stick. The wolves fled but the boy was astonished to see that in the midst of the pack, a young, wild-haired naked girl fled with them on all fours.

When the boy told his parents what he had seen, they were not sure whether to believe him. Soon other shepherds and cowboys began reporting the same strange girl. The Indian scouts from Camp Hudson also saw her, and from then on they refused to go anywhere near Devil's River.

Many of the local ranchers felt an attempt should be made to capture The Wolf Girl so she could be brought to the safety of civilization and live a normal human life. So a hunt was launched in 1851. The trackers found the hand and footprints of *La Niña de Los Lobos* among the tracks of a pack of wolves. When the hunters caught up with the pack, several fast-riding *vaqueros* chased the animals, and the girl, into a box canyon. The wolves had no difficulty escaping up the steep, rocky slopes, but the girl, who was slower and not built for scrambling like the canines, was quickly lassoed and brought to the ground.

The Wolf Girl screamed like a woman, howled like a wolf and fought furiously as her captors struggled to bind her wrists and ankles. She was taken to a nearby ranch, where she was untied and locked in a shed. While the ranchers tried to decide what to do next, the terrified girl began to howl mournfully. Soon answering calls came from the darkness beyond the ranch.

When The Wolf Girl heard the howling of her pack, she went berserk. The ranchers could hear her throwing herself against the walls. They realized if she were not restrained, she would injure herself badly. Ropes in hand, the men cautiously opened the shed door. In an instant, the girl flashed past them and ran back to the wild world from which she had come, never to be recaptured.

She was seldom sighted after that, since she was undoubtedly more wary than ever. The last to report seeing her were members of a railroad surveying crew who caught a glimpse of her in 1852. When and where she eventually died remains forever unknown; her body was never found.

But 139 years later, The Wolf Girl, or someone like her, showed up again.

One day in the fall of 1974, three bowhunters from Dallas went javalina hunting north of Del Rio. As evening approached, they pitched a camp near the banks of Devil's River. One of the sportsmen, Jim Marshall, hiked off to the river's edge to gather firewood in the twilight. Minutes later, he came running back, white-faced and scared.

"If I tell you what I just saw, you won't believe

me," he gasped. "You've got to see this for yourselves. C'mon!" He led his friends hurriedly down to the river and looked around. "She's gone," he said nervously. "There was a skinny, naked, long-haired girl down on all fours digging in that anthill over there. Where'd she go? Wait... there she is! On that sandbar!"

The three astonished men stared in amazement; even though the light was fading, they could see The Wolf Girl clearly. There seemed to be a faint, white aura around her as if she was, as Marshall said later, "in a haze, a kind of foggy mist." When The Wolf Girl looked up and saw the hunters, she vanished instantly, only to reappear a few seconds later several yards further downstream.

A chill ran up Jim Marshall's neck. "You know what I think? I think this would be a good night to stay in a motel." The bowhunters hastily took down their tent, stuffed it in their car and headed off to Del Rio, leaving the ghost of The Wolf Girl to prowl her dark domain alone.

One can understand why some ghosts apparently choose to stay forever in a certain place; The Wolf Girl surely would never be happy anywhere else, nor wish to live in any other way. But occasionally, it is hard to comprehend why certain spirits constantly appear in a specific setting and behave in a totally inexplicable manner. One such Texas case involved a ghost seen repeatedly by Viola Tollett in 1913.

Viola and her husband, Henry Tollett, were a young Black couple who lived in a small house out in the mesquite country about 20 miles from Uvalde. Henry was a cowboy, a skilled brush country roper who, like his father, Alf Tollett, worked for a nearby ranch. Naturally, his work kept him away from home a good deal of the time. But Viola was not too lonely since her mother-in-law, Betty Toulett, lived within walking distance.

The two women were drinking coffee in Viola's kitchen one morning when an odd-looking man walked up to the open front door and peered inside. He was the strangest looking fellow either woman had ever seen, dressed like an old-time frontiersman. His raccoon skin cap, his buckskin shirt with fringe on the sleeves, and his tattered leather leggings gave him the appearance of a figure returned from a bygone era.

As soon as he realized the women had noticed him, he started to enter the house. Very quickly, Viola and Betty dashed out the back door and ran away. From what they considered to be a safe distance, they watched as the silent, mysterious man walked away from the house and plodded up the brushy hill beyond, moving upward through the chaparral and prickly pear until he could no longer be seen.

When Henry came home a few days later, Viola told him at once about the curious visitor. "It musta jest been yer imagination," Henry concluded.

Viola shook her head. "I didn't imagine him. Yer mama seen him, too."

In the morning, Viola and Henry were out in their backyard when the same oddly dressed man came around the corner of the house. "That's him!" Viola cried. "Right over there. Look!"

"What you talkin' about, woman?" Henry asked. "I don't see nobody."

"He's lookin' right at us, and he's a-comin' this away."

"Viola," Henry said firmly. "There ain't nobody there." But the weird, anachronistic man continued to approach the couple. As Viola clutched her husband's arm, the apparition passed by her so closely she briefly had direct eye contact with him. His gaze was neither malignant nor threatening, and his mouth was curved in a very slight smile, as if he was thinking: "I know you can see me." He went on up the hill again and waded through the spiny brush until he was out of sight.

In the weeks that followed, Viola saw the ghost again on several occasions. His behavior was always the same; he would simply walk past the house and climb the hill. Viola never saw him come back down and Henry never saw him at all.

One spring morning, Viola paid a visit to a neighbor, an Hispanic woman named Maria. As the two women sat and talked in the front room, they heard a horse approaching the house. Maria went to the door, looked out and immediately crossed herself and began to pray.

Puzzled and frightened, Viola also looked out. She, too, began to tremble. The rider loping toward Maria's home was the same buckskin-clad man she had seen before on foot.

Not far from the house there was a large, deep hole which Maria's husband had dug because he had heard rumors of gold having been buried on his property by the previous owner. The horseman rode to the edge of the pit and paused momentarily. Then he spurred his horse and plunged directly into the hole. Both Viola and Maria could hear rocks clattering and dirt falling as the rider disappeared from view.

Viola exhaled a deep breath. Finally she said, "I'm gonna go take a look." Cautiously she stepped across the yard to the still-dusty pit. When she peeked over the rim, there was no one there.

After Viola returned to the house, Maria asked, "You saw nothing, *es verdad?* Neither have I, although

I, too, have looked. This has happened many times since my husband dug that hole. The man we just saw comes out of nowhere, rides into the hole and vanishes. I don't know how or why."

Now Viola was completely confused. What did it all mean? Had the digging disturbed this spirit away and caused it to return? Why was it seen only in daylight? Weren't ghosts supposed to come out at night? Why was the phantom always on foot when it went up the hill near Viola's home and always mounted on a horse when it went into the hole at Maria's home? And why, she wondered, was it that only women could see the apparition? Why was it invisible to men?

Since Viola Tollett could answer none of those questions, she decided the only smart thing to do was just stay out of the ghost's way whenever it appeared to perform its strange ritual.

She was lucky in one respect. She could at least see the ghost that haunted her property. It is much more difficult to live with invisible phantoms. A classic example of an unseen supernatural presence which defied explanation is the tale of the Pebble Throwing Ghost of Peach Tree Village.

This annoying poltergeist frightened and perplexed a pioneering family named Fortenberry throughout the many years they lived in their sturdy log house beyond the outskirts of the little East Texas village of Peach Tree. The Fortenberry's home was a typical frontier cabin, simple yet strong and comfortable. Its walls were of native pine; the double-slab puncheon floor was smoothly hewn and the fireplace is said to have been large enough to hold a six-foot log. The peaked, cedar-shingle roof extended out over a narrow porch upon which the family could sit and enjoy the coolness of the evening.

The new house still smelled of fresh pine and cedar wood when the Fortenberrys moved their meager belongings into it in the late 1850s. R.L. Fortenberry hung his rifle on a pair of deer horns on the wall while his wife positioned the rawhide-bottomed chairs in the living room. After they tucked their two little daughters snuggly beneath the homemade quilts on their beds, the young parents settled back to contentedly watch the flames curling around the log burning warmly in their new hearth.

It was nearly midnight when the Fortenberrys were startled out of their reverie by what sounded like a fairly heavy stone striking the roof and clattering down the shingles. As the now-alert couple listened intently, two more stones hit the roof and bounced away. Then, within less than a minute, a whole fistful of pebbles splattered against the shingles and rattled off.

Fortenberry took his rifle down from the wall, cracked open the door and glanced out. He could see no one near the cabin. He bolted the door, and stacked the rifle within easy reach before returning to a restless sleep.

When morning came, he searched for footprints in the sandy soil around the house. He found none, nor did there seem to be any disturbed stones on the premises. That night, at almost precisely the same time and in exactly the same way, the phenomenon repeated itself: first one large rock landed on the roof, then two more thumps were heard followed by a cascade of pebbles.

This time the noise woke the two little children. They sat up and cried out, shivering fearfully in their beds when Fortenberry came in to comfort them. "There's got to be a natural explanation. It's probably just the shingles creakin' as they cool off," he assured.

In the morning, he climbed up onto the roof to re-nail all the shingles. Still, that night they all heard the same worrisome sounds again.

The Fortenberrys often invited their neighbors over to listen to the strange noises. Everyone heard them, of course, but no one had an explanation. One night several men hid themselves in the trees around the cabin in hopes of seeing the pebble thrower. Although the sounds were repeated right on schedule, neither the rocks nor the thrower were seen.

As time went by, the Fortenberrys got used to this odd nocturnal event; even the girls came to realize they need not fear the ghostly noises. Everyone around Peach Tree would have loved to solve the mystery, but no one ever did. The old cabin is long gone now, and the pebble thrower, who cast those invisible stones for more than 50 years, is also gone forever.

Texas ghosts, like most, seem to have a repetitive behavior. For reasons unknown to the living, they come back time and again to compulsively repeat the same performance. But there are some occasions when a ghost will show up just once, never to be seen again. Usually these apparitions appear for some very imporant reason, such as to deliver messages from the Spirit World.

Josiah Wilberger and Sarah Hornsby shared a supernatural experience of this sort even though they were miles apart at the time.

On a hot August day in 1883, Wilbarger was riding with four companions through the oak covered hills on the outskirts of Stephen F. Austin's American colony in Mexico's Texas. These five men, Wilbarger, Strothers, Christian, Standifer and Haynie, were searching the countryside for lands suitable for a settlement. In the middle of the morning, as they crossed a sunlit clearing, they saw a lone Comanche warrior sitting on a horse, watching them.

According to historic accounts, the exploratory party chased the Indian and may have fired a shot or two at him. If so, it was a very stupid thing to do.

Stephen Austin, a very diplomatic man, had made peace with the fierce Comanches; there was a truce between the Indians and the White settlers as long as neither side provoked the other. Now Wilbarger's group had deliberately and senselessly violated that agreement.

They rode on until noon at which time they dismounted and began eating their midday meal. Suddenly a barrage of gunfire and a shower of arrows flashed out of the trees. Strother was killed instantly, while a rifle ball broke Christian's leg. As Wilbarger ran to help his fallen friend, he took an arrow in the leg.

Haynie and Standifer managed to reach their horses and mount up, just as Wilbarger received a second arrow through his other leg. He was limping desperately toward his horse when a rifle shot struck the back of his neck. It burst from his throat in a spray of blood. Haynie and Standifer saw Wilbarger fall. Feeling certain he was dead, they galloped madly away as the Comanches dashed out of the woods with their scalping knives in hand.

But Josiah Wilbarger was not dead. His bullet wound had temporarily paralyzed him, so he seemed lifeless and could not move a muscle. But he was aware that his head was being pulled up by the hair and that he was being scalped alive. After the Indians left, he passed out completely.

Hours later, he was awakened by excruciating pain. The first sound he heard upon regaining consciousness was the horrifying buzzing of a swarm of blowflies feeding on the open wound on his head.

The Comanches had stripped Wilbarger of his boots, so he was able to tug off a sock. He shooed away the flies and pulled it over his mutilated scalp. He was extremely thirsty but he knew water would not pass down his torn throat. He tried to get to his feet, but his now swollen, arrow-pierced legs would not hold him up. Slowly he began to crawl.

The nearest cabin, the Hornsby place, was more than six miles away. Wilbarger had covered no more than a few hundred yards before he realized he could never make it. He dragged himself to the base of a tree, leaned against its trunk and waited to die.

Night fell. Wilbarger grew steadily weaker. His body was growing numb. Then he heard a gentle voice speak his name. He managed to turn his head and look up. He saw his sister standing beside him.

"You're not going to die, Josiah," she said. "I'm going for help. Just rest, Josiah. You're going to live." She smiled and faded into the darkness.

Josiah Wilbarger had not seen his sister since he left their hometown in Missouri years ago. His pain-stunned mind could not imagine how she found him, but her appearance renewed his hope for survival. He knew she would save him.

Standifer and Haynie had reached the Hornsby cabin several hours earlier. They told Rueben and Sarah Hornsby about the ambush and said that Stother, Christian and Wilbarger were all dead. The Hornsbys gave the traumatized survivors refuge for the night. After all had bedded down, Sarah Hornsby had a dream.

The dream was so vivid that it woke her. She sat up in bed and shook her husband's shoulder. "Josiah Wilbarger's alive," she said when he opened his eyes.

"A woman just came to me in a dream. She said he's hurt real bad and we should go to him at once."

Rueben Hornsby shook his head drowsily. "He can't be alive, Sarah. You heard what those two boys told us. The Comanches killed him. Now go back to sleep."

Sarah lay back on her pillow. Before long she dozed off and the dream re-occurred. This time, Sarah insisted that Rueben get out of bed. "That woman spoke to me again," she said. "And she showed me where he is. He's sitting on the ground, leaning on a tree not far from Christian's and Strother's bodies."

Sarah glanced out the window. "It'll be daylight soon. You better wake those other boys and go find poor Mister Wilbarger."

Within an hour, three very skeptical men rode off toward the dawn. When they reached the ambush site, they found Josiah slumped against the thick trunk of an oak tree, just as Sarah had said they would. Carefully, they lifted him onto a horse and as gently and quickly as possible, they took him back to the Hornsby's cabin.

Sarah dressed his wounds and cared for him until he was strong enough to return to his home in Bastrop.

It was there that he received a letter from Missouri informing him that his sister, Margaret, was dead. She had died just one day before she made her miraculous appearance in Texas to save her brother's life.

Josiah Wilbarger lived for another 12 years, until 1845 when he tripped and struck his fragile, exposed skull on a low beam in the doorway of a cotton gin. He was originally buried in Bastrop where his mansion with its pillared porches and towering chimney still stands. In 1932, Josiah Wilbarger was reburied in the Texas State Cemetery in Austin beneath an engraved memorial stone which honors him as one of Texas' most unique early pioneers.

In Texas, ghosts sometimes seem as common as armadillos. Nearly every town, every cemetery, and every dark, secluded place seems to have been visited at least once by one type of supernatural entity or another.

Yet as haunted as the entire state of Texas is, there is one area that is more haunted than any other part. The rugged Chisos Mountains of Big Bend National Park are so crowded with legendary ghosts that they deserve a separate chapter.

Bibliography - Chapter 3

Blakely, Mike. *True West.* Austin, Texas. Western Publications. October, 1987.

Dearen, Patrick. *True West.* Austin, Texas. Western Publications. December, 1990.

Fenley, Florence. *Frontier Times.* Austin, Texas. Western Publications. Winter, 1958-1959.

Murray, Earl. **Ghosts of the Old West**. New York. Dorset Press. 1988.

Sems, Verne. *Frontier Times.* Austin, Texas. Western Publications. December-January, 1979.

Tevis, Dean. *Frontier Times.* Austin, Texas. Western Publications. December-January, 1979.

Wilbarger, J.W. **Indian Depredations in Texas.** Austin, Texas. Hutchins Printing House. 1889.

4

Haunted Crags
of the Chisos

The gods must have been angry when they created the Chisos Mountains. They must have clawed at the land, gnawed on it until they stripped it to the quick. When their anger finally subsided, they simply abandoned the starkly carved landscape and let the ages complete their work.

The gods surely knew that time is the ultimate sculptor, and that slowly but surely the awesome geologic wonder they had unearthed would be honed to perfection, standing against the sky forever as the centerpiece of the raw, desert land now known as Big Bend.

The Chisos Mountain Range is a fairly small but very bold outdoor gallery of carefully arranged natural works of art, a collection of scowling buttes, fang-like pinnacles and jagged peaks. It is also an ideal habitat for scores of ghosts.

49

Even the name "Chisos" is, as the National Park Service points out, "usually interpreted as meaning 'ghost,'" although no one seems able to agree on the origin of the word.

There is archival proof that the mountains were called *Los Chisos* by the early Spanish explorers in spite of the fact there is no such word as *chiso* in Spanish language dictionaries. "Ghost" in Spanish is either *fantasma* or *espíritu*. It is possible that *chiso* may be a corruption of *hechizo*, the Spanish word for "bewitched." It is said that when the Spaniards first saw these mountains, they were shrouded in mist... the range may well have looked very ghostly and bewitching.

A more likely explanation of the mountains' name is that it was derived from a mispronunciation of an Apache word. At the time of the Spanish arrival, the Chisos were an Apache stronghold. These Indians called themselves *Chishi*, meaning "people of the forest." Perhaps, due to the spooky nature of the mountains, the name Chisos gradually became associated with the word "ghosts" and remains so to this day.

In any event, it is certainly a fitting, if not correct, interpretation of this haunted landscape's name. No visitor to Los Chisos can deny that this place has a definite sense of enchantment about it. The odd illuminations so often seen on the peaks are reason enough to make one expect to see ghosts.

Frequently, on nights after a rain, the mountains will light up with a phosphorescent glow. At other times during the night, entire valleys have been known to suddenly become as bright as noon for a few minutes before darkness returns.

The eeriest Chisos light, however, is the one referred to as the Ghost Torch. This tiny spot of light travels horizontally at night along the crest of a high, stony ridge. Legend has it that the light is a torch carried by an Indian ghost who guides the spirits of the dead to the Afterworld. A natural explanation has been suggested for this strange light: it may be that as the stars rise one by one from behind the ridge they give the impression of being a single light moving steadily across the rim of the ridge.

Many who have seen the Ghost Torch do not accept this theory; they insist it is just one light which occasionally vanishes momentarily during its journey as it passes behind the sharp crags of the serrated skyline.

Who knows? Sometimes mystery, like beauty, is in the eye of the beholder.

Strange sounds also have been heard in these spell-bound mountains. Most puzzling is the ringing of the bells. Time and again, travelers in the Chisos have reported hearing the distinct, unmistakable and rhythmic clang of church bells deep in the mountains, miles from the nearest church. One of the best, most detailed accounts of an occurrence of this phenomenon was made by an Alpine area resident, Ferdinand Webster, in 1927.

On Good Friday of that year, Webster was riding horseback with three friends on a mountain trail which crossed an open Chisos valley. It was a quiet day; there was not a breath of wind. The sky was clear and the four men were riding silently and contentedly with the Texas sun warm on their shoulders. All at once, out of the blue, a bell rang. A single, deeply-toned note reverberated across the empty, brush-choked countryside.

The riders paused with a bewildered look on their faces. They glanced around and listened hard. The bell rang again. And again. Then silence returned.

Webster, who was leading a pack mule behind the others, swung down from his saddle. "Maybe the mule's riggin's loosened up," he said. "Probably a strap buckle's bouncin' on that skillet I tied on top." He checked the mule's burden only to find everything still tightly secured. Next Webster picked up a small rock and tapped the skillet. It produced nothing but a dull thud.

"That ain't it, Ferd," one of his buddies said. And as he spoke, the bell began ringing again. For several minutes the bell tolled in the wilderness. When at last it stopped, the four mystified men rode on. They urged their horses up onto a ridge to search for a place to camp for the evening.

As twilight closed in, they began unloading their gear. Suddenly one of the four men, Vivian Lujan of Marfa, dropped the blankets he was carrying and pointed excitedly at the hillside across from their camp.

"¡Madre de Dios!" he blurted. "Do you see that? ¡Es los espíritus de los Chisos!"

Lujan's companions peered into the dusk, and they, too, were astounded by what they saw. About three quarters of a mile away, two silver-white, flare-like flames stood on the brushy slope. From that distance it was difficult to judge their size, but Webster estimated them to be about three feet tall and one foot wide.

Then Lujan gestured to the south. "¡Mire!" he shouted, "Look over there!" Two more flames had risen. One was red and the other green. They seemed to be approximately the same height as the first two flares, and they remained visible throughout most of the night.

Upon his return to Alpine a few days later,

Webster told the local priest, Father Palomo, what he and his friends had seen and heard.

The priest nodded knowingly. "There have been others who have had the same experience," he said. "And always during Lent. Some believe the flames are divine candles and the bell is a heavenly bell which rings to bless the souls of the many people who died in the mountains.

"On the other hand," the priest said with a coy smile, "it may be the bell rings to remind people that they should be in church on Good Friday, not out riding around the mountains on horseback."

Whether or not Father Palomo was right in his pious explanations of the phenomena, he was definitely correct about one thing: a lot of people have died in the Chisos.

In the early 18th Century, a large group of Spaniards were slain in the vicinity of Lost Mine Peak. There are two versions of what happened. One has it that these avaricious men of New Spain had enslaved a sizeable number of Indians, taken them into the Chisos and forced them to labor in a silver mine. The Indians eventually rebelled and managed to kill their captors.

The second version claims the Spaniards were working the mine themselves when they were attacked by Indians. They tried to flee but the Indians chased them down and killed them one by one. Regardless of which story is true, the ghosts of these men can still be seen sometimes on moonlit nights, running desperately from crag to crag, forever trying to escape their pursuers.

Another ghost who appears frequently is that of Apache Chief Alsate. In 1882 the last of his tribe was living in the Chisos. They were few in number by then, but they were still a defiant people who often fought the

soldiers of Mexico and raided Mexican villages. On one
of these raids, Alsate's band rode into a trap. When
they attacked the village of San Carlos on the southern
bank of the Rio Grande, a vastly superior Mexican force
was waiting for them. A surprise barrage felled many of
the Apache warriors. The rest, including Alsate, were
encircled and captured.

Leonecio Castillo, commander of the Mexican
troops, ordered Alsate to stand in front of an adobe wall
to face a firing squad. It is said that just before the trig-
gers were pulled, Alsate vowed to return. Not many days
afterward, sheepherders and *vaqueros* in the Big Bend
area began reporting sightings of Alsate's ghost.

He was seen most often silhouetted against the
sky, high on the rocks above his former stronghold.
Alsate, being an Apache, was a nomadic man, so it is
not surprising that his ghost has appeared in many
places throughout the Chisos and in the nearby Sierra
del Carmen. However, most of the sightings have been in
the vicinity of Casa Grande peak. This, coincidentally,
seems quite appropriate since, when Casa Grande is
viewed from just the right angle, a rock profile of a
fierce-looking man is visible. The ghost has shown up
here so many times that the rock formation is sometimes referred to as Alsate's face.

Some of the Chisos ghost stories are sad and
poignant tales about people who were driven by terrible
circumstances to commit acts of utter desperation. Their
deeds were so horrifying that their anguished spirits will
always haunt the places where these tragedies occurred.

Once, long ago, a young Indian woman gave birth
to her first child on a night when the moon over the
Chisos was full. She knew this was a bad omen for
babies born in moonlight are in grave danger of being
cursed and transformed into animals. The next morn-

CASA GRANDE PEAK, towering above its haunted kingdom.

Photo by the author

ing, the worried mother was sitting in front of her wicki-
up with her baby in her arms when a six-legged lizard
ran across her foot. Now she knew for certain that her
worst fears were about to become a reality. There was
only one thing she could do to prevent her baby from
being changed into a demonic reptile. With tears streaming down her face, she carried her tiny infant up to the
crest of Cold Water Cliff, held it out over the edge, closed
her eyes and opened her hands. The baby screamed as
it fell until it abruptly stopped. The young mother huddled down in the rocks and wept for hours.

The baby's cry and the mother's sobs are still
heard in the Chisos. Those who claim to have heard
these sounds are usually scoffed at by those who have
not heard them. One of these scoffers was a cowhand
named Isidoro Salgado. To him, the story was nothing
but a simple *leyenda*, a quaint, folkloric legend.

But one night in 1954, Salgado and his brother-
in-law were tending a herd of cattle near Cold Water
Cliff. They had bedded down on the ground for the night
and were nearly asleep when their horses began to
behave nervously, as if they sensed something the men
did not. Almost simultaneously, a baby's voice shrieked
in the darkness.

Both men threw off their blankets and jumped to
their feet. As their horses pawed the ground and pulled
at the tethers, they heard a lonely wail of a sobbing
woman echo down from the cliff.

Isidoro Salgado shivered. "I have never believed in
ghosts," he said. "But now that we've heard this, I know
the old legend is true."

Many others who have doubted the old Chisos leg-
ends have become believers after unexpected encounters
with the mountains' ghosts. One ghost in particular is
probably more startling and shocking than any other to

those who come upon it without warning. This apparition is not seen often since few people visit the distant waterhole it haunts. Still fewer people know the ghost's sad and tragic story.

More than a century ago, a beautiful young woman whose name is no longer remembered lived with her widowed father on a large ranch in northern Chihuahua. One day a savage gang of *bandidos* raided the ranch, killing the father and servants. The gang seized the daughter and took her on a long, hard ride to a waterhole deep in the Chisos.

Here the *desperados* pulled her from her horse and threw her down in the dust. She rose to her feet, saying, "I know what you are going to do to me. At least let me bathe first." She waded out to the deepest part of the tepid pool of water, exhaled deeply and submerged. Before the *bandidos* realized what she was doing, she had deliberately drowned herself.

The cursing outlaws left her body in the lonely waterhole. Some folks claim she is still there today. Over the years, a number of people said they saw her floating face down in the water. Those who have tried to wade out to her always created ripples that caused her image to shimmer away. Like nearly all of the Chisos ghosts, she remains everlastingly just out of reach.

Actually a few of these mountain ghosts seem to be trying hard to make contact with the living. They beckon mysteriously to anyone who chances upon them. During the 1940s, a cowboy from a ranch near Terlingua was riding alone through the Chisos when he heard a woman's voice call out to him. Looking up, he saw her standing on an overhanging cliff, high above the canyon floor. The cowboy always described her as "lookin' just like an angel without wings." The woman's hair flowed around her face on this windless day while she raised her arms and motioned gracefully for him to come up to her. The astonished cowboy declined the invitation and rode off swiftly in the opposite direction.

When he got back to the bunkhouse, he told his saddle pals about his experience. Everyone derided him until one oldtimer spoke up. "Don't laugh, boys," he said. "I once seen somethin' stranger'n that out there in those damn Chisos."

As he rolled a cigarette, the old cowboy told of the time when he had ridden out into the mountains in search of a horse that had strayed from the ranch. Near Burro Mesa he saw a lone man sitting on a rock.

"I hollered at him," the cowboy said. "I asked him if he'd seen a little bay horse. He got down off the rock and waved at me to come over to him. So, I did, but when I got up close to him, I seen he weren't a man at all. He was a ghost. His face was all pale and his eyes had a kinda glow to 'em."

"He said to me, 'Forget about the horse. Follow me and I'll show you somethin' much more interestin.' Well sir, I done the same as you, sonny. I high-tailed it out of there just as fast as I could."

One can only speculate about what these men would have encountered had they followed these phantoms. The Chisos hold so many secrets that in all probability most of them will never be revealed. Even so, the mountains hold plenty of mysteries which are not supernatural.

About 30 years ago, a strange discovery was made here. A very unusual, out-of-place artifact bearing an enigmatic message from the distant past was found quite by accident. It became what may be the earliest mystery in the history of the Big Bend Country.

How to Visit the Haunted Chisos Mountains

From the Visitors' Center and Park Headquarters at Panther Junction, drive west three miles to the Basin Junction and turn left. Five miles up the Basin Highway, one comes to the Lost Mine trailhead. This 2.3 mile trail passes through the part of the mountains where the ghosts of the Spaniards have been seen. Deservedly, this scenic trail is one of the most popular in the Chisos.

Another fine trail with a history of Alsate sightings is Boulder Meadows Trail. This pleasant three-mile walk wanders through the piñon-juniper woodlands to a grassy flat covered with huge volcanic boulders. A number of designated backcountry campsites are located along this trail for those who may wish to experience the enchantment of a Chisos Mountain night.

Bibliography - Chapter 4

Aiken, Riley. **Ghosts of the Chisos.** Dallas, Texas. Southern Methodist University Press. 1970

Dearen, Patrick. *True West.* Austin, Texas. Western Publications. December 1990.

Gipson, Fred. **Cowhand.** New York. Harper & Brothers. 1948.

Miles, Elton. **Chisos Ghosts.** Dallas, Texas. Southern Methodist University Press 1972.

5
Big Bend's Mystery Tablet

The Rio Grande twists like a snake along the border between Texas and Mexico. It drifts and surges through the romantically named canyons it has carved —Santa Elena, Mariscal and Boquillas. Other lesser streams flow down to join the mighty Rio —Terlingua Creek, Juniper Canyon and Tornillo Creek.

Near the spot where Tornillo Creek enters the river, a very different type of water comes forth from the limestone and shale rock formations. This highly mineralized "fossil water" was deposited more than 20,000 years ago and is heated geothermally to 150 degrees F by igneous rocks deep in the earth.

These healing waters have soothed countless generations of health seekers. Tourists have been coming to this remote pool for nearly a century to sweat out their impurities, inhale the steamy vapors and drink the mineral-rich water. Before the Anglos came, the Spanish and the Mexicans enjoyed the hot springs. Still earlier, the Indians benefited from this gift given

61

them by the Earth Mother.

But these visitors were not the only ones to come to this distant place. There were others as well. A long, long time ago, an intrepid group of travelers passed through this sun-baked land. These wayfarers had journeyed an incredible distance before reaching the Rio Grande, but no one would even know they had been in the land that would be known as Texas until nearly 2,000 years later.

During the time when the Indians were the only inhabitants of the Big Bend, they marked the grey shale cliffs with red pictographs near the hot springs. The other ancient travelers from so far away also left a mark of their passage, a poignant message that would go unnoticed and unread for centuries.

Throughout human history of the Big Bend hot springs, few of its visitors stayed long. Thousands of people from many races and cultures have come here like pilgrims to a miraculous shrine, but no one settled permanently at the springs until 1909. In that year, Joseph Oscar Langford brought his family to Texas from Mississippi. At the time, Langford was in very poor health after having suffered through many bouts with malaria. When he heard about the therapeutic springs, he immediately bought the land sight unseen and headed for Big Bend.

Along with his wife, Bessie, and his two young daughters, Lovie and Lucille, Langford camped in an open area just above the river. Each morning for 21 consecutive days, J.O. Langford walked down the cane-shaded path beneath the overhanging cliffs, stepped down the natural stairways of limestone slabs and eased himself into the hot, medicinal water.

At the end of three weeks of daily baths and many glasses of mineral water, Langford's health was restored. He felt vigorous once again and was now full of ideas. "These waters made me well," he told Bessie. "I want to build a spa so others can come here and be cured just as I was."

With the help of Mexican laborers, Langford first built an adobe house for his family. Then he hired stone masons to construct a bathhouse over the springs while he built a long, cane stalk-covered *rama-da* nearby to provide a shady camping place for his visitors. As word of Langford's spa spread, he did, indeed, host many guests from both sides of the border. Joseph and Bessie heartily welcomed everyone, although they did make one firm request: any patient suffering from a "social disease" had to bathe in a special, separate tub.

The Langfords charged the bathers ten cents a day to use the springs or $2 for the full 21-day treatment which, of course, J.O. Langford highly recommended. The transplanted Mississippians were doing modestly well until 1913 when the Big Bend Country abruptly became a very dangerous place to live.

Gangs of *bandidos* calling themselves *Los Banderos Colorados*, the Red Flaggers, began terrorizing both sides of the Rio Grande. These savage outlaws thundered across the land with blood-red banners flapping above them. The flags symbolized the gang's ruthlessness, making it horrifyingly clear that they gave no quarter and took no prisoners. Small troops of United States Cavalry patrolled the long border as best they could, but the land was far too vast to be made safe.

The Langfords knew it would be only a matter of time before their defenseless spa would be targeted by *Los Banderos Colorados*. Reluctantly, they abandoned their home and moved to El Paso. Within a few years, turbulent West Texas calmed down. Although law and order was restored, J.O. Langford continued to work in El Paso until he felt he had saved enough money to build a real resort on his rough piece of land in the Big Bend. In 1927, he directed the construction of a durable stone store and post office. Alongside this stalwart, twin-chimneyed building, he replaced the by-then tumbled down *ramada* with a long row of motel rooms. The white, stuccoed interiors of the rooms were all decorated with brightly colored murals painted by Mazie Lee, an artist from Marathon.

In the front of the store, stood a hand-powered gasoline pump. Near the cliffs, Langford built a grassless miniature golf course. The Langfords were justifiably proud of their unique riverside resort, so J.O. promoted it like a showman. He had leaflets printed up and made sure they were distributed far and wide. The irresistible flyers promised:

"Health at Hot Springs. Hundreds have regained their health by drinking and bathing in this wonderful water. Why not you?

"Sufferers from asthma, kidney, liver and bladder diseases, dropsy, jaundice, pellagra, eczema, rheumatism of all forms, stomach troubles including ulcers and indigestion, alcoholism and tobacco poisoning, hiccough, boils, skin diseases, influenza, sunburn and genito-urinary diseases have left their troubles here and gone home rejoicing.

"Hot Springs is an ideal winter resort, warm sunny days. Very seldom freezing temperatures. Splendid fishing the year round. Catfish range from ten to fifty pounds. Good hunting grounds and magnificent scenery."

In addition to being an enterprising entrepreneur, J.O. Langford was a collector and a craftsman. In and around his store, he displayed ancient metate grinding stones, arrowheads and flint knives along with carefully carved and polished wooden oddities that he fashioned from tree branches and roots.

There was a variety of interesting things to see at the Langfords' health spa, but the most fascinating object of all was completely hidden away in a crevice so inaccessible that even J.O., in his endless and thorough explorations of his property, never chanced upon it. If he had been the one to discover the Big Bend Mystery Tablet, it would certainly have become the most talked about item in his extensive collection of unusual objects.

The Langfords operated their popular health haven until 1942 when they retired and sold the hot springs to the State of Texas. The State, in turn, ceded it to the federal government for inclusion in Big Bend National Park. Maggie and H. Baylor Smith ran the aging resort under a Park Service concession contract until 1952.

After the Smiths left the site, it deteriorated rather quickly. The bathhouse had already been almost completely destroyed by floods; the motel veranda collapsed; the murals faded. The spring continued to flow as always, but the tourist traffic was down to a trickle.

Then in January 1962, four casual sightseers came to the hot springs to hike around a bit. Within an hour, they found what the American Epigraphic Society would later call "one of the most significant archaeological discoveries of the century."

Charles and Bernice Nickles were two transplanted Texans who operated a floatplane service in Alaska. Every winter, the Nickles came "outside" to the "South 48" where they basked in the warm Texas sun at the San Marcos home of their son, Donald Uzzell and his wife, Reva.

The four of them set off one bright winter morning for an extended weekend in Big Bend. After spending the night at the lodge in The Basin, they headed off to take a look at the hot springs. The weather was pleasant so once they had inspected the old buildings, the two couples decided to take a short hike. They crossed Tornillo Creek on stepping stones and walked past the scowling cliff face above the opposite shore.

Glancing up, Donald Uzzell said, "Look at that. There's a cave up there. Can you see it?" When the others peered and squinted and shook their heads, he said, "You've got to look from just the right angle. Come over here by me. Now do you see it? You know, I think I could climb up to it. Wouldn't it be something if there were pictographs in that cave? I'll be right back."

With the others urging him not to try it, Uzzell began to scale the unstable rocks. Almost everything he touched was loose and crumbly, ready to fall away. But after a few suspenseful minutes, he reached a height of 30 feet and squeezed himself into a crevice which from below looked like a mere shadow on the cliff wall.

His wife and parents could hear him clattering around inside the niche. Soon his voice echoed out of the limestone wall: "I've found something! Dad, can you climb up part way? There are some things I want to hand down to you."

Hesitantly, Charles Nickles inched his way up to within reach of his son who handed him a small slab of dried clay inscribed with curious symbols. "Be careful," Uzzell said. "It's really fragile. There are about six more stacked up on a ledge in here."

Nickles passed the slab on to Bernice who had

also come up aways. She, in turn, handed it to Reva standing on the ground. One by one all the slabs were removed from the cave. When everyone was down safely, they spread Uzzell's findings out on the ground.

The pieces fit together like a jigsaw puzzle to form a single, long tablet covered with 13 lines of mysterious writing. Realizing they had stumbled onto something which might be of major importance, everyone agreed the tablet should be turned over to the Park Service. Uzzell photographed the stone before placing the pieces carefully in the trunk of his car. The four excited tourists headed off for Panther Junction Ranger Station.

The ranger to whom they showed their discovery was openly skeptical. The Uzzells and the Nickles could tell by the amused expression on his face that he thought they were playing a joke on him. He must have thought the four of them had created the tablet out of river mud.

"Well now," the ranger chuckled. "This sure is interesting. But bein's ya'll are the ones who found it, why don't ya'll just keep it? Go ahead. Take it on home with ya."

Had the foursome known what the eventual fate of the tablet would be, they undoubtedly would have accepted the ranger's offer. Instead they insisted that the artifact be examined by Park Service archaeologists. Without much enthusiasm, the ranger promised to have that done. He dutifully jotted down the Uzzell's phone number and swore he would get back to them.

Several months passed. The Uzzells heard nothing from the Park Service, and their phone calls to the park headquarters were never returned. At last, two years later, a letter from the ranger arrived informing the Uzzells that "the men who inspected the tablet pieces were unable to learn anything from them."

Now the disappointed couple realized if the riddle of the Big Bend Mystery Tablet were ever to be solved, it would be up to them to find someone who would take the stones seriously. Donald called the venerable Texas historian, J. Frank Dobie, to ask if he might know of someone who could translate the tablet. Dobie suggested an imminent epigrapher named Lewis R. Church.

The Uzzells sent a color print of Donald's photograph of the rock to Church who in turn passed it on to Dr. Leo Phillips of the Classical Languages Department at Brigham Young University. Both men agreed that some of the characters appeared to be similar to very ancient Greek, but there were too many dissimilarities for them to make a translation.

Next, the Uzzells contacted two amateur epigraphers, Bernice and Jack McGee, who had written several magazine articles on pre-Columbian inscriptions found on rocks in Oklahoma and elsewhere. The McGees immediately became intrigued and wanted very much to see the actual tablet.

Their prompt inquiries to the park headquarters put them in touch with Rollin Wauer, Big Bend's chief naturalist. Wauer expressed genuine interest in the enigmatic photograph and assured the McGees he would do his best to find out what had become of the slabs. A few days later, he reported back with devastatingly bad news.

A search of park records revealed no mention of the tablet. The ranger who had accepted the pieces of clay from the Uzzells had since been transferred to Nevada. When Wauer called him, he said he did remember the tablet.

"It lay on the floor of the maintenance building

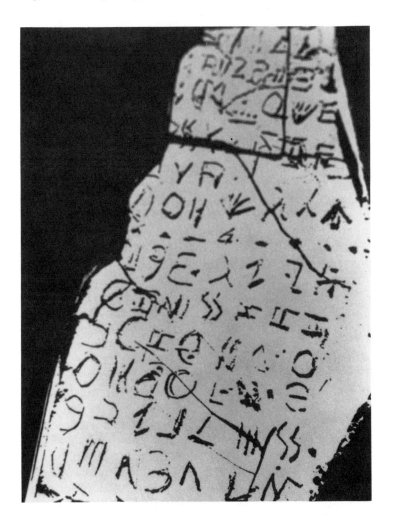

BIG BEND'S MYSTERY TABLET. Its plaintive message went unread for 2,000 years.

Photo by Donald Uzzell

for months," the ranger recalled. "I showed it to any and all that were willing to look at it, but everybody agreed it hadn't any antiquity nor historical significance. It disintegrated from all that handling and, when we moved it down to the new administration building, it turned into a pile of dust."

The McGees and the Uzzells were shocked and nearly crushed by this disheartening disclosure, but they refused to give up. They still had the photograph, so they continued to mail it out. The renown historian Cyclone Covey, received a copy, as did a professor of classical languages, John Andronica.

Covey wrote the McGees to say the inscription appeared to be authentic: "If the tablet were a hoax, Andronica and I would have spotted it at once. If the inscription were pure classical Greek, we could translate it, but there is another language mixed in the Greek letters. A lot of non-Greeks, both pagan and Christian, wrote Greek, including Phoenicians, Egyptians, Jews and Irish monks."

Covey then made a suggestion: "It might be worthwhile to go back to the find-site and re-explore the cave. It's not impossible that there may be additional artifacts that were overlooked during the first visit."

So in October of 1970, almost nine years after the tablets was originally brought into the light of day, the Uzzells and the Nickles, accompanied by the McGees and Rollin Wauer, returned to the hot springs. Donald Uzzell re-enacted his climb and thoroughly re-examined the narrow niche. He found nothing.

Next, Bernice McGee made the precarious ascent. Her hands were smaller than Donald's, allowing her to probe the thin, dark cracks between the multi-layered limestone strata of the cave's walls. She, too, found nothing. It was now firmly established that the photograph was the only proof that the tablet had ever existed.

Cyclone Covey continued to study the photograph. He consulted with other epigraphers, including Barry Fell, president of the American Epigraphic Society. Through these combined efforts, a translation finally began to emerge.

The inscription was extremely complex, a rich potpourri of mingled languages. It was written not in Greek, but in a variant of Libyan alphabetic script with repeated refrains in Lycian and Lydian. The lines of characters traversed the tablet in curious ways. The first four lines read from left to right while the section below the horizontal fracture was written in boustrophendo-style, going from left to right as it began but switching back to right to left on the following line. Each phrase alternated in this way down the length of the tablet.

Voyagers from the ancient kingdoms of Lycia and Lydia in West Asia Minor and Libya in northern Africa sailed daringly back and forth across the Mediterranean for hundreds of years before the birth of Christ, trading goods, knowledge and skills. They were superb mariners, so it seems inevitable that they would challenge the greatest sea on their side of the world — the Atlantic.

If they succeeded in reaching the New World, it seems logical that they would have traveled inland via the rivers. It can also be assumed these explorations were terribly arduous, fraught with perils and extreme hardships.

Therefore, it is not surprising that the first two sentences on the Big Bend tablet read: "Why this suffering? Oh, what anguish."

The message on the sun-baked clay is in the form of a prayer to the sun god Mithras asking for his divine intervention into their sorrowful lives. Three times the words, "Heal us" are repeated in the text.

Mithras was a Persian-Iranian deity who revealed himself to an Iranian prophet named Zoroaster some time around 1100 BC. Under Mithras' guidance, Zoroaster founded a religion known as Zoroastrianism which taught that the world is the scene of a never-ending conflict between Ormuad, the force of good, and Ahriman, the force of evil. Ormuad represents life; Ahriman brings only death.

Zoroastrianism thrived in the Mediterranean countries for centuries and later became the basis for the original Jewish and Christian dogmas with their concepts of a benign God and a malignant Devil.

If Zoroastrians actually journeyed to ancient America, what country did they come from and when? Barry Fell thought it was probable they sailed from Iberia on the Spanish peninsula, since a few Iberian artifacts have been found in lower Mississippi, an indication that Mithraic sun worshippers once ventured ashore on the Gulf Coast.

This meager archaeological evidence shows the Zoroastrians may have been here as early as 100 B.C., so it is possible the Big Bend tablet was 2,000 years old when it was discovered.

Since the tablet's inscription is a prayer begging for healing, it is hard to believe it was mere coincidence that the Zoroastrians wound up at a medicinal hot springs. But, how did they find this obscure place? Were they guided to it by sympathetic paleo-Indians, or was it pure chance? Did they see a cloud of hot vapor rising on a chilly morning as they drifted past these bleak rocks and then draw into the shore to investigate it?

Or perhaps it was Mithras himself who showed them the way.

In any event, one more unanswered question remains: were the tablet-makers healed by this wonderful water? Did these sufferers "leave their troubles here and go home rejoicing," as J.O. Langford's customers did?

If so, it seems likely they might have made a second tablet, inscribed it with a prayer of thanks, and tucked it away in another niche somewhere high in the foreboding cliffs that guard this precious gift of water from the earth. Unless and until such a second tablet is found, the enigma of the Big Bend Mystery Tablet has no final ending.

How to Visit the Mystery Tablet Find-Site

From the Panther Junction Park headquarters, drive southeast toward Rio Grande Village for 17 miles to the hot springs junction sign. Turn right (south) onto a very rough dirt road and go slowly for 1.9 miles to a parking area near the old hot spring store and post office.

Tornillo Creek flows past the parking lot and the old buildings on its way to the Rio. Above its opposite bank stands the crumbling cliff where the tablet was found. Climbing these unstable rocks is strongly discouraged. A better idea is to walk down to the hot springs, soak in these allegedly miraculous waters, and contemplate the fate of the ancient mariners.

Bibliography - Chapter 5

Fell, Barry. **Saga America.** New York. Times Books. 1980.

Langford, Joseph Oscar. **Big Bend: A Homesteader's Story.** Austin, Texas. University of Texas Press. 1973.

Littlejohn, Margaret. **Hot Springs: The Fountain Ponce de Leon Failed to Find.** Big Bend Natural History Association. 1981.

McGee, Bernice and Jack. *True West.* Austin, Texas. Western Publications, Inc. July-August, 1972.

6

Ghost Birds & Mothmen

Texas has always had its fair share of strange creatures. After all, any state that can claim an animal as unlikely as an armadillo should be capable of coming up with almost any type of unusual creature. From the giant lizards of prehistoric times to the rare albino buffaloes of the frontier days and the incredible longhorns of the open ranges, Texas has hosted a wide variety of fascinating animals.

But all of those Texas beasts are perfectly natural; their actual existence is undeniable. It is the other category of weird creatures —the ones which are from no known species and whose existence cannot be proven scientifically— that is the most intriguing. Some very, very odd animals have shown up in Texas over the years. Their appearances are always so sudden, unexpected and infrequent that they don't allow themselves to be studied. All of these truly astonishing creatures are winged, though many are not birds.

One that does resemble a bird is the so-called Ghost Bird of Fort Stockton. This manifestation is said to rise, phoenix-like, occasionally from some crumbling adobe ruins behind the old Spanish church. The Ghost Bird is nocturnal, luminous and has a wingspan of 36 feet. It never flies or moves about; it simply wavers in the darkness until it fades away.

The Ghost Bird rose many times in Fort Stockton's early days, often enough that the local school children (undoubtedly the same ones who watch for *La Llorona*) formed the habit of going out at night to wait for it. Apparently they were not too terribly frightened by this awesome apparition, probably because it never tried to chase them. Nevertheless, the youngsters took prudent precautions. They always went out in groups and never ventured closer than 36 feet from that towering Ghost Bird.

A much more worrisome nighttime creature was the Texas Death Bird, a harbinger of death which flew to places where someone was doomed to die in the very near future. Here it would commence its eerie hooting making its announcement of impending tragedy. The Death Bird was an owl of medium size, had long, slender wings and appropriately, was jet black. This in itself made it unique since there is no species of black owl in all of North America.

The Death Bird has been sighted countless times

in the wooded regions of central Texas where it was both feared and grudgingly respected. The devilish bird's prophesies always came true. Whenever the owl hooted, someone inevitably died at that exact spot.

It seems as if just about everyone in old time Texas had a Death Bird story to tell. One of the most ironic of these tales was the one told by Issac Motes in 1871.

Motes was a Texas Ranger assigned to a small detachment stationed near Albany to protect the scattered settlements strung out through what is now Shackelford County. It was a nearly impossible task for the frontier was in almost constant turmoil. The Comanches had been moved to reservations in Oklahoma, but they frequently rode back into Texas on raids, plundering farms and stealing horses.

In June of 1871, informants within the Comanche Nation brought word to the Rangers that a raid was being planned. It would be a sweeping, lightning fast attack when the moon was full. The Rangers' commanding officer, Lieutenant Nolan, glanced up at the crescent moon above him and realized he would need reinforcements as soon as possible.

He immediately dispatched one of his Indian scouts, a Tonkawa called "Indian Jim," to Forth Worth to rally the Rangers there. Jim was Issac Motes' best friend; the two of them had ridden many trails together. Motes clasped his friend's hand, wished him godspeed, and watched him thunder off to the horizon.

Indian Jim had a very fast pony, and it was assumed he could reach the Fort Worth Garrison within three days and return in no less. After a week went by, neither he nor the reinforcements showed up in Albany. Motes grew very worried. Reports had filtered in indicating that a number of Comanches had already been sighted skulking around the countryside seeking out vulnerable farms and choice herds of horses. It was possible Jim had run into trouble.

Motes requested permission from Lieutenant Nolan to go in search of his friend and to make sure the message had gotten through to Fort Worth. With time running out, Nolan readily agreed. Motes rode off at once.

The horseman traveled swiftly through the dense timber south of the Clear Fork of the Brazos, staying within the protective cover of the drooping branches and over-hanging vines. The weather was taking a turn for the worse; even though it was only late afternoon, the landscape was darkening under blue-black storm clouds. Motes decided it would be wise to pitch an early camp.

He chose a level spot near the tangled roots of a tall, stately oak. He was just starting to unroll his rain slicker when a black owl flew into the upper branches of the tree above him to perch before letting out a mournful hoot.

A chill ran up Issac Motes' back. Though he could scarcely see the dark bird against the blackening sky, he knew it was the Death Bird. It was announcing that an inevitable and unescapable death was about to occur on the ground at the base of this tall tree.

Numb with fear, the Ranger began gathering up his gear preparing to flee. When a great bolt of lightning ripped the sky, Motes saw the evil bird spread its wings and swoop away. Moments later, from the corner of his eye, Motes caught a glimpse of a human being moving through the brush a few hundred feet away.

Although the figure was visible for only a couple of seconds, Motes could tell by the long braids that it was a Comanche who had undoubtedly picked up his trail and followed it to his camp. Hastily, Ranger Motes drug his saddle to the roots of the oak, placed his rolled up slicker behind it and covered it all with a blanket. In the dim light, it vaguely resembled a sleeping man. With his rifle in his hands and his Colt revolver tucked in his belt, Motes scooted backwards into the shadows. Each time the lightning flashed, he scanned the woods. Twice, he saw the approaching Comanche and each time the Indian had moved a little bit closer.

During an especially vivid lightning strike, Motes sighted a second Indian slipping in from the opposite direction. Now he knew he was caught between at least two Indian warriors, and that he could retreat no further since his back was above a steep-walled, clay-sided gully which he could not enter and cross without knocking down noisy showers of rocks. He crouched lower and waited.

Lightning again whitened the clearing. Motes heard an arrow thud into his saddle. Stealthily, the Comanche emerged from the brush with his bow in his hands. Simultaneously, the second Indian rose and fired a rifle bullet into the tall warrior's heart, slamming him against the trunk of the post oak. The Comanche slumped down and died in a sitting position.

After the thunder rolled away, a voice called out, "Issac! Where are you?"

Motes could scarcely believe his ears. It was Indian Jim. He crawled out of his hiding place, grinning widely. "Jim! You saved my life! How did you find me?"

"I was scouting ahead of the Forth Worth Rangers when I smelled your horse," Indian Jim replied. "The Rangers are about an hour behind me. We should all reach Albany late tomorrow afternoon."

Motes stared at the arrow embedded in his saddle.

He raised his eyes to the highest branches of the oak tree. "I saw the Death Bird, Jim," Motes confided. "It was right up there, at the top of that tree, hootin' at me. I figured I was a goner because that bird is never wrong, is it? If it says somebody's gonna die, somebody dies."

Indian Jim nodded solemnly. "That's true. And that Comanche should have been listening."

Whether or not the Death Bird still wings its diabolic way across the night skies of Texas is uncertain. If it does, it may well go unnoticed and unheeded as it flits along today's brightly lighted skylines. But there are other creatures poised out there in the darkness, making appearances that cannot be missed if one is in the right place at the right time. One of the most inscrutable entities is the creature dubbed, "The Mothman."

Sightings of a creature resembling a human moth have come from around the world throughout history, but in recent times, some of the most dramatic and highly improbable sightings were made in Texas. The earliest report of a Texas Mothman was published in the *Houston Chronicle* on June 18, 1953.

The incident took place in Brownsville on a hot summer night at the home of the Walker family. The Walkers had stayed up unusually late and were sitting on their front porch talking to friends, when, at 2:30 a.m., a huge shadow appeared on the lawn about 25 feet away. Hilda Walker's first impression was that it was "the magnified reflection of a big moth caught in the nearby street light. Then the shadow seemed to bounce upward into an old pecan tree."

Leaning out cautiously over the porch rail, Walker saw "the figure of a man with folded wings standing on a branch." She pointed him out to her companions, and they, too, saw this unbelievable sight. Later, each of them described what they had seen in identical terms.

The winged man, they said, had a dim light all around him, making him clearly visible. He was tall, perhaps over six feet, dressed in skin-tight dark grey or black clothing and quarter-length boots. Although he swayed with the branch, he seemed to be perfectly balanced. The moth-like person paid no attention to the human beings gawking at him from the porch, but he glanced about sharply, dunking and bobbing his head as if he was lost or confused.

Thirty time-frozen seconds passed before the gauzy aura faded out. Then the dark figure shot straight up out of the tree without undraping its wings. An instant later, the Walkers heard "a "loud swoosh over the housetops across the street."

No one else witnessed this incredible event, undoubtedly due to the lateness of the hour. This made the Walkers wonder if their Mothman sighting might not have been an isolated incident. Could it be that, late at night, this creature or others like it, suddenly appear and abruptly vanish when there are few people awake to see them? If so, where do they come from? And where do they go?

The Walkers' description of the winged person in the pecan tree was precise and detailed, but it was quite different from the next Mothman to be sighted in Texas. On New Year's Day, 1976, two young girls, Tracey Lawson and Jackie Davis, ages 11 and 14 respectively, saw "a horrible-looking, big, black bird about five feet tall with wings bunched up over its shoulders. It had a gorrilla's face, mean, red eyes, and a thick, ol' beak about six inches long."

This awful monstrosity was seen by the two youngsters as it stood in the twilight in a plowed field on the outskirts of Harlingen. It was approximately 100 yards away when Tracey Lawson observed it closely through her father's binoculars. For more than ten minutes, the creature remained completely motionless. Then it flashed upward without opening its wings and was gone.

The girls went with their parents to the field, and there they found a pair of three-toed tracks, eight inches across, pressed into the ground.

By an incredible coincidence, on that same night, January 1, 1976, Doctor Brenhold Schwarz reported seeing "an enormous bird" near Great Notch, New Jersey. It was airborne with is huge wings extended, but it seemed to be gliding, since as the doctor noted, "its wings didn't seem to be flapping much at all. What disturbed me most was it was so white, even as dark as the sky was. I know this sounds ridiculous, but it was luminous."

One week later, on the edge of Brownsville, 26 miles southeast of Harlingen, Alverico Guajardo heard something hit the side of his mobile home. He opened the door and saw a hideous, four-footed creature sprawled out on the ground, stunned by its collision with the trailer. It had sleek, black feathers, bat-like wings spreading out from its shoulders, a long beak, and blazing red eyes. It glared at Guajardo and emitted a high-pitched hissing noise as it scuttled away into the shadows.

The next sighting of a Mothman —or "Birdman" as some preferred to call them— was made in broad daylight near Poteet, 36 miles south of San Antonio on January 11. On that day, two ranchers encountered a five-foot bird standing in a water tank. As they approached it in their pickup truck, it took off into the air without flapping its wings.

The repeated appearances of these unidentifiable "birds" took a sinister turn on January 18 at 10:30 p.m. when a Raymondville resident, Armando Grimaldo, claimed to have been attacked by one. Grimaldo said he heard a flapping of strong wings accompanied by "a strange whistling sound." He went out into his backyard. When he stepped into the darkness beyond the porch light, something pounced on him, seizing one of his legs with a pair of powerful claws.

Grimaldo fought wildly, kicking and striking the shrieking beast. The monster was about five and a half feet tall with a wingspan of ten or 12 feet. It had "a monkey-like face, large red eyes and beak, and dark, leathery skin without feathers." Grimaldo managed to tear himself loose and raced back to the house. Once inside behind a locked door, he saw that his pantleg was shredded. His leg was only bruised by the creature's crushing grip.

Throughout the rest of January 1976, sightings of Mothmen and "big birds" continued to be reported in southern Texas. A "cat-faced bird with six-foot wings extending from each side of its five-foot long body" was seen by a motorist driving a country road near Olmito on January 18. The following afternoon, an extremely tall bird with a six-inch beak was seen by Homer and Marie Hernandez as it stood beside an irrigation ditch at San Benito. Two days later, Francisco Magallanez of Eagle Pass told of being chased by the biggest bird he had ever seen.

One of the oddest aspects of these reports is that a variety of creatures were being described; no two were exactly the same. The Brownsville Mothman was humanoid and wore clothing, while others were feathered and some were leathery. Frequently they had mammals' faces, sometimes with beaks, sometimes without. The only thing they all seemed to have in common was a reporting of bright, red eyes.

Yet, inexplicable as these creatures were, even weirder things were cruising the Texas skies that mysterious winter 20 years ago. On January 18, three San Antonio elementary school teachers were carpooling to work near the city when a huge, flying reptile swooped past their car. The early morning light was slanted so that one of the teachers, Patricia Bryant, "could see the skeleton of this bird's wings, and it stood out black against the grey skin." Her fellow passenger, David Renden, also confirmed the bone structure of the creature's wings and noted that it was gliding rather than flying.

When the teachers arrived at school, Renden said, "This is going to sound crazy, but I think I know what that thing was." With the others, he hurried to the school library. He excitedly thumbed though an encyclopedia, and then pointed to a picture of a pteranodon. "That's it, isn't it?" he asked. The others nodded.

About four weeks later, on February 24, Libby and Deany Ford saw a "big, bat-like bird" near Brownsville. They, too, identified it as a pteranodon from a picture in a book on paleontology.

Pteranodons, or pterodactyls as they are also called, were the largest flying creatures of all time; their membranous 25- to 50-foot wings carried them through the skies of prehistory for 30 million years. They had three-foot long, toothless beaks and two-foot long bone crowns extending backwards from the bases of their skulls.

These spectacular denizens of the air were gliders rather than flyers. It is believed they may have flapped their wings during takeoff or may have run on their stubby, three-toed feet to launch themselves over the edge of cliffs. Regardless of how they did it, the pteranodons soared unchallenged over the inland seas, swooping down to scoop up fish.

The existence of pteranodons in Mesozoic Texas was proven in 1975 when Douglas Lawson, a graduate student from the University of California, uncovered the fossilized skeleton of one in Big Bend National Park. But, the pteranodons had been extinct for 130 million years. How could they possibly be reappearing in Texas?

Of course, many people believed all of these sightings were simply misidentifications of large, but ordinary birds such as albatrosses, condors or cranes. Albatrosses seemed unlikely candidates; although they have seven-foot wingspreads and can glide as well as fly, they are rarely seen east of the Pacific Coast. Condors, with their 10-foot wingspans, were an even more questionable explanation since, by the 1970s they were nearly extinct in North America; their habitat had been reduced to a small area in the mountains of southern California.

Cranes, it seemed, were the most logical explanation. Sandhill cranes are common from Canada to Mexico. They are tall with seven-foot wingspans, and interestingly, have red caps on their heads which could conceivably be mistaken for red eyes. However, cranes do not have animal faces or leathery skins, and they do not take off without spreading their wings. Nor do they attack people in the middle of the night.

So if conventional birds are ruled out, one is left with a choice of two conclusions: either some mighty strange things were roosting in Texas in 1976, or all 19 of the widely-separated witnesses were lying or hallucinating.

The Texas "flying creature flap" generated

enough publicity to attract two very talented paranormal investigators to the state in February of that year.

Jerome Clark and Loren Coleman had co-authored several books on unexplained aerial phenomena; Clark was associate editor of *Fate* magazine.

Together, they interviewed all of the witnesses and found them to be, without exception, honest and reliable people who genuinely believed they had seen inexplicable phenomena. They could offer no explanations, but they were convinced that what they had seen was real.

Clark and Coleman could not find explanations either, but they were able to come up with some thought-provoking theories. First, they acknowledged the obvious fact that Mothmen and creatures from the prehistoric past could not possibly be permanent residents in the contemporary world. Such huge, startling curiosities would certainly be continuously seen, would be followed, and their habitats would be located. Clark and Coleman suggested these creatures may be apparitional —primordial ghosts that haunt an area briefly before they vanish. Or perhaps, they have returned to this world through some sort of time-warp, through a space-time window of the fourth dimension.

"We ought not under any circumstances take our theories too seriously, and we must never give them greater primacy than we give the observed facts," Clark later wrote. "In my darker moments, I have come to suspect that unexplainable aerial phenomena may represent something so far beyond us that our attempts to understand them may be comparable to an ant's efforts to comprehend the principles of nuclear physics."

A bit of an exaggeration, perhaps, but there are

baffling phenomena that occur which today's limited scientific knowledge cannot explain. It may well be that strange creatures do come and go in this small biosphere called Earth. Where they come from and where they go cannot be determined; the only certainty is that they will continue to be seen from time to time.

One such creature came back to Texas in 1983. On September 14, James Thompson was driving an ambulance back from South Padre Island to Harlingen when he saw a bird-like creature sailing the sky not far from his vehicle. It was close enough that he could estimate its body length at eight to ten feet, and each of its wings were "as wide as the ambulance and seemed to be about an inch thick, like a shark's fin."

Thompson said the creature was not feathered, but had a greyish, roughly-textured, hide-type covering. The amazed driver pulled off on the shoulder of the road and "just watched him fly away."

How many times unbelievable creatures have flown, seen or unseen, across the wondrous skies of Texas, no one can say. But in Texas, it's always worth keeping an eye on the sky, both by day and by night. One never knows what may show up next.

Bibliography - Chapter 6

Bord, Janet and Colin. **Alien Animals**. London. Granada Publishing. 1980.

Dearen, Patrick. *True West*. Austin, Texas. Western Publications. December 1990.

Motes, Issac. *Frontier Times*. Austin, Texas. Western Publications. October 1923.

Story, Ronald D. **The Encyclopedia of UFOs.** New York. Dolphin Books. 1980.

Vaczek, Louis. **Life Before Man.** New York. Time-Life Books. 1972.

7
Witchcraft: Black & White

Witchcraft has long had a strong influence on Hispanic culture in Texas. Its ancient roots run deep, spread far, and firmly grasp any bodies and souls that come within reach of its spell.

Witchcraft followed Texas' earliest settlers up from Mexico where it was practiced by the Indians long before the Spanish arrival. The Spanish invasion of Mexico brought European fears of Satan and his demonic minions to the new land along with medieval ways of dealing with these insidious threats. On both banks of the Rio Grande, a special type of supernaturalism evolved, creating a complex folk wisdom capable of coping with both the good and the evil aspects of these powerful forces.

Those with even passing knowledge of witchcraft know that it comes in two forms: "white," which should be embraced, and "black" which must be resisted in all ways possible. Related to "white magic," are the traditional healing practices known as *"curanderismo,"* which has benefited Hispanic people of Texas enormously for many generations.

Some *curanderos* are folk healers of near-mythic abilities. Their extensive knowledge of herbal remedies and natural cures are unexcelled in this part of the world. Since some also claim to be able to see into the spirit world, *curanderos* can often give practical and protective advice to people living in the constant presence of the supernatural. Some *curanderos* attempt to undo hexes and spells cast by practitioners of black witchcraft.

One man who influenced the development of contemporary *curanderismo* more than anyone else was a charismatic, self-trained botanist who called himself "*El Niño Fidencio*." Born in 1898 and raised in poverty in Nuevo Leon, Fidencio as a young man received a "call from God" to serve humanity as a healer and teacher. He traveled widely throughout Mayan Guatemala and rural Mexico learning the ancient folkways. Although he had very little formal education, he became a great botanist with a thorough knowledge of more than 200 medicinal plants.

In the late 1920s, El Niño Fidencio established a spiritist healing center in a *barrio* in San Antonio. Here, in a room glowing with candles, Fidencio performed many miraculous cures over the years, dressed in a Christ-like robe of Guadalupe blue.

After his death in 1938, this folk saint's spirit is said to have supernaturally assisted more than 50 other *curanderos* from Florida to California, and as far south as Guatemala. One of the best of these "chosen vessels" was another San Antonio resident named Juan Luís Martinez.

Martinez was a remarkable man in many respects. Not only was he a powerful *curandero*, he was also a fiery labor organizer, a socialist, and a firm believer in equal rights for women. He walked confidently with one foot trodding through the radical reality of his time, the other touching down in the misty realm of spiritualism.

Martinez was a believer in reincarnation; to him, death was merely a transition to another life. He taught his followers that they had already lived many lives, sometimes as a man, sometimes as a woman. Martinez always stressed the importance of living one's current life in an exemplary manner. If one lived a good and caring life, the next life would be a still better one. But if one lived a life of sin, an extremely unpleasant reincarnation could be expected.

As if it were not enough for Juan Luís Martinez to be a very gifted healer, a revolutionary thinker and a believer in the eternal continuity of life, he also claimed to be a medium. Many spirits were channeled through him: the two most prominent ones, he said, were Benjamin Franklin and St. John the Baptist. With two such powerful advisors guiding him, it is no wonder that Martinez was one of Texas' greatest *curanderos*. Great *curanderos*, both men and women, usually come from humble backgrounds, and often do not fully develop their marvelous talents until midway through their lives. One such late bloomer was a highly respected Rio Grande Valley *curandera* who came to be called Doña Felicia. When Felicia was a child of six or seven, she had a little dog of which she was very fond. One day, her dog was run over by a car. She found him lying dead in the street. Sobbing uncontrollably, she carried her beloved pet to the curb and cradled his lifeless body in her arms.

Her mother rushed out to console her, and Felicia cried, "How could God of let this happen? How can

He be so cruel! If God is good, as you say He is, He will bring my doggie back to life."

She buried her face in the dead dog's fur and, as her tears fell, the animal began to stir. Soon it stood up on all four legs, alive again, wagging its tail, and licking the tears from Felicia's smiling face.

Word of the miracle spread quickly through the community, leading many visitors to her door to see the little girl and her dog. One of the visitors was an elderly woman carrying a very sick-looking chicken. "Could Felicia cure the chicken?" the old woman asked. Hesitantly and without the faintest idea of what to do, the girl took the drooping bird in her hands. As she did so, she "felt," rather than heard, a voice within her saying, "Look in the chicken's throat."

Felicia pried open the chicken's beak and saw a fish bone. Using tweezers, she carefully removed the bone and the chicken instantly had a wing-flapping recovery. Now more people than ever began visiting Felicia.

Some brought sick animals with them, while others had ailments of their own. By rubbing these sufferers' foreheads with her little hands, the child discovered she could relieve the pain of headaches, stomach disorders, menstrual cramps and colds.

Felicia's mother did not know what to make of all this, so she sought the advice of a priest. After the holy father had listened to Felicia's story, he nodded. "Yes," he told the mother. "She has the gift all right, but she is much too young to be using such power. Your daughter has no understanding or knowledge of *curanderismo*. She could easily make an innocent mistake which could cause harm to someone, or she could even injure herself. I believe it is much too dangerous for her to continue healing at such a tender age."

The mother took the priest seriously and ordered Felicia to cease healing people and animals. The girl dutifully obeyed and resumed her normal, carefree childhood. The years passed quickly. Soon Felicia was a grown woman who rarely thought about the miraculous days of her youth. One day, while she was talking to one of her aunts who was a *curandera*, she told her about her memories of the gift she had once used.

The aunt grew very excited. "You must use your gift, Felicia," she said. "You must learn *curanderismo*. I will teach you all that has been revealed to me, and you will be able to begin healing again."

Felicia became the older woman's apprentice, studying the mysterious healing arts for many months. She memorized all the right prayers, learned how to bless water, and to know which herbs had curing powers. She studied illnesses and how they manifest themselves. Before long, Felicia felt her old powers returning, but still she lacked confidence to treat anyone other than family members or close friends.

Her husband was a migratory worker who followed the harvests north each year. One night, after a hard day's work, he went to bed, fell asleep and never woke up. Felicia was stunned by her husband's sudden death, but then she felt the voice speak within her again.

It said: "I have taken your husband to free you so you can use your gift. You have not used it freely so far because of your other obligations. I have sent you no children, so now you are free to cure and remove evil from the world. Share your blessing with others. Through you, I will cure."

After a long, prayerful period of mourning, Felicia built an altar in her living room, surrounded it with holy statues, crucifixes, ornately framed religious

paintings, racks of votive candles and bouquets of flow-
ers.

Here, for the rest of her life, Doña Felicia welcomed any and all sufferers who knocked on her door.

Most of those who sought her help were poor
people who could give little in return for the miracles
she performed. They brought her chickens, baskets of
vegetables or, if they had one, a dollar bill. "I cure for
love, not to get rich," Doña Felicia often said. "My
reward is being close to God."

If *curanderos* are close to God, then their oppo-
sites, the practitioners of black witchcraft, may be
regarded as allies of Satan. The use of supernatural
powers for evil intent is acquired through a *pactado
con Diablo*, a pact with the Devil, which commits a
person to a lifetime and an after-life of service to the
Evil One. It also allows one to do things no ordinary
mortal can.

Witches can fly, turn into animals, or become
invisible and listen secretly to peoples' conversations.
They possess the evil eye which can make a victim very
sick with just a stare. Worse yet, witches cast spells
and put hexes on their victims, causing serious illnesses and terrible misfortune.

The evil that witches do can be undone, of
course. Spells can be broken and supernaturally
induced sicknesses can be cured. Witchcraft can be
confronted... *if* the witch can be identified. And therein
lies the problem.

The world of witchcraft is shrouded in secrecy.
Witches make themselves known only to each other
and those who wish to hire them. When a bad-hearted
person desires the services of a witch, there is no need
for that person to go in search of one; a witch will come
to them. Witches know intuitively when someone needs

their dark talents, and they are always willing to commit evil deeds for a price.

Once a witch puts a hex on an unsuspecting victim, the bewitched has little chance of breaking the spell unless he or she can figure out who cast it. That is not an impossible task, as the following story shows.

Elsa and Roberto were newlyweds, very much in love. One morning as Elsa was sweeping the porch, she saw a strange black cat coming across the yard toward her. The animal was pretty obviously a stray, and looked very hungry. Elsa set out a plate of scraps which the cat eagerly devoured. That night, Roberto and Elsa had their first argument.

It was a bitter quarrel. Roberto was shocked at his gentle wife's sudden and uncharacteristic vehemence. She shouted at him, called him names and even used profanity. Then, she slumped on the couch, trembling and crying, unable to believe she had exploded the way she had.

When morning came again, so did the cat. It quickly licked up the dish of leftovers Elsa set out for it and scurried away. In the evening, Elsa picked another fight with Roberto. She raged at him, yelled and screamed, and threw her coffee cup at the wall. Then, as before, her fury subsided as quickly as it came. She fell on the couch sobbing in dismay.

Each night, Elsa experienced wild mood swings which always left her exhausted and terrified. After a week of enduring his wife's tirades, Roberto began avoiding them by putting on his hat, slamming the door, and heading for the nearest *cantina*. Elsa realized if she could not regain control of herself, she would ruin her marriage. Knowing she needed help, she went to a *curandera*.

After listening to Elsa tell about her inexplicable

behavior, the old woman grew very serious. "You have been bewitched, Elsa," she said. "Someone who wants to destroy your marriage has hired a witch to put a hex on you. It may be one of your husband's ex-girlfriends, or it could be one of your old boyfriends.

"Yes, someone has sent a witch to your house. But I doubt that the witch comes as a human being. It is more likely that she transforms herself into an animal. A dog, perhaps, or a cat."

Elsa's eyes widened. "A cat has been coming to my house every morning since my troubles started. It's a stray so I felt sorry for it, and I've been feeding it."

"Elsa," the *curandera* said emphatically. "You must drive that cat away and make sure it never returns. That is the only way to break the spell."

Elsa went trepidaciously back to her home. As expected, the cat was waiting for her beside the food dish. She filled the dish with leftover breakfast beans. As the cat ate, Elsa cautiously backed to the wood pile, selected a sturdy stick, leaped forward and smacked the cat with a hard, rib-cracking blow.

The startled animal screamed in a shrill human voice and bounded out of the yard as Elsa pelted it with stones. Next, she took off her crucifix and laid it across the food dish.

The cat never came back, but Elsa's sunny disposition did. She and Roberto were blissfully happy once more.

Witches do not necessarily need to disguise themselves as animals to perform their wicked deeds. They can enter an unsuspecting person's life in any human form they choose. This can make it even more difficult for the witches' victims to identify their tormentors. An undetected witch can cause a tremendous amount of harm, sometimes to an entire family.

An all-too-typical example occurred in the Rio Grande Valley not too many years ago. A young man named Tomás met a beautiful woman at a dance. After a brief courtship he married her. Within a matter of weeks, Tomás was killed in a car wreck. His wife, Angela, who was with him in the car, was uninjured.

The young widow had no other friends or family to turn to, so Tomás' grieving parents, Rosa and Rafael, pitied her and invited her to move in with them. Shortly thereafter, a series of further misfortunes took place.

Rafael severely injured his hand on the job. The wound refused to heal and became so badly infected he could no longer work. Rosa began experiencing excruciating headaches. Oddly, her flock of chickens began dying one by one for no apparent reason. One night, Rosa and Rafael awoke to find the house filling up with smoke; they ran from their bedroom to discover the living room sofa burning.

None of this seemed to bother Angela particularly. In fact, she appeared to be quite indifferent toward her benefactors. She spent most of her time watching television and never offered to pay board and room or help with household chores.

Finally, one evening after supper, when Rosa was suffering from a headache, she asked Angela if it was expecting too much for her to at least help with the dishes. Angela was appalled. "I am a guest in your home," she shouted. "And I expect to be treated like one!" The two women began arguing. Angela became so incensed she slapped Rosa with her open hands. To defend herself, Rosa grabbed a knife off the kitchen counter and slashed at Angel's flailing arms, drawing blood.

When Rosa saw the blood running down Angela's

forearm, she gasped in horror. The blood was not red! It was dark, thick and greasy.

"Oh, my God," Rosa cried out. "You have the blood of a witch! You are a witch! Jesus, Mary and Joseph, save us!"

Angela reacted to the sound of the holy names as if she herself had been slapped in the face. She shrank back, stumbled to the door and fled into the night, never to be seen again.

Once Angela was out of their lives, Rosa and Rafael quickly recovered. Rafael's hand healed nicely, Rosa's headaches went away, and no more chicken died. The couple was left to always wonder who Angela really was, and whether she had somehow caused the death of their son.

The utterance of holy names is said to be one of the best defenses in a direct confrontation with a witch. In fact, they can be used effectively during encounters with several witches at the same time. To unexpectedly face one witch is bad enough, but to be surrounded by them, as sometimes happens, can be a terrifying experience. This, a young fellow named Carlos learned on a summer's night in South Texas some time ago.

Carlos was a shy and awkward little man who worked at a low-paying, common labor job. He had few friends, and the local girls always found an excuse to say "no" when he asked them for a date. One evening, as Carlos sat morosely in a bar, a tall handsome stranger in a dark suit sat down beside him. He struck up a conversation. After a few minutes the stranger noted, "Carlos, you seem unhappy. Is something troubling you?"

"Yes," Carlos confided. "I am unhappy. No one in this town respects me. I am treated like dirt."

"That should not be," the stranger said sympathetically. "You deserve respect. But to gain it you must have power; you must become more powerful than those who belittle you." He paused thoughtfully for a moment before saying, "I have some very powerful friends, Carlos. I think you'd like to meet them. Why don't I introduce you to them tomorrow night?"

It was nearly midnight the next evening when Carlos excitedly accompanied his new friend to the edge of town. A little further down he road, they entered a dark ravine where Carlos was surprised to see a small house located on the arroyo floor. He had passed this ravine many times in the past but had never noticed a house there before. And, he thought, what an odd place to build one.

The interior of the dwelling was brightly lit. Through the windows, Carlos could see many men and women playing musical instruments and dancing with wild abandon. His tall companion knocked on the door.

"Who is there?" asked a voice from within.

"We are two," the tall man answered. "One is ignorant."

A shaft of light fell over Carlos as the door opened. With his friend's hand on his shoulder, he entered the house. The frenzied dancers paid no attention to him as he gawked at them. Some were very old and ugly while others were young and very beautiful. Suddenly the dancing stopped and all eyes turned to the door.

A large, foul-smelling goat walked into the room on its hind legs. It approached each dancer in turn and paused while that person knelt and kissed its tail. Once the goat had circled the room, it returned to the darkness outside.

Next, an enormous snake slithered in. It, too,

made its way around the room, rearing up to eye level in front of each person, allowing itself to be kissed on its flickering tongue. Soon the serpent raised itself in front of Carlos' face. Carlos' companion whispered in his ear. "This is the kiss of wisdom. Kiss the snake, Carlos."

The young man trembled with fear and revulsion as he stared into the snake's black, unblinking eyes. "No!" he shouted. "In the name of Jesus, Mary and Joseph — no!"

Instantly he found himself standing alone in the darkened ravine. Everything had vanished, the house, the witches and goat and the snake. Only the pungent odor of sulphur lingered in the air. Carlos ran non-stop all the way back to town and never again did he talk to strangers in a bar.

Such stories are not uncommon in certain parts of Texas where witchcraft is an eternal part of life. The ever-present threat of black magic haunts the darkness, elusive, largely unseen but very menacing. Of course, a lot of people nowadays scoff at the old tales and try to dismiss them as folklore. Still a large segment of our society continues to maintain a belief in, and a fear of, the Devil. So if in the minds of many, the Evil One still prowls the land, who can say with certainty that the witches do not follow?

Bibliography - Chapter 7

Madsen, Williams. The **Mexican Americans of South Texas.** New York. Holt, Rinehart and Winston. 1964.

Seth, Ronald. **Witches and Their Craft.** New York. Newhouse Press. 1968.

Simmons, Marc. **Witchcraft in the Southwest**.

Flagstaff. Northland Press. 1974.

Velimirovic, Boris, **Modern Medical Anthropology in the U.S.-Mexican Border Population.** Washington, D.C. Pan American Health Organization. 1978.

West, Stanley and Macklin, June. **The Chicano Experience.** Boulder, Colorado. Westview Press. 1979.

8

Madstone Magic

Life on the early Texas frontier was one of constant peril. Sudden death could come at any time. Every subsistence farmer in his isolated "dog-run" cabin, and every cotton planter and field worker knew each day that dawned could very well be the last, for him or some member of his family.

Rattlesnakes and Indian arrows, tornados and frigid "blue northers" could strike without warning. Expectant mothers could never be sure that they would survive childbirth or that their colicky babies would live. In this vast, sparsely settled land where doctors were few and far between, diseases such as typhus and typhoid fever took a heavy toll.

Death on the frontier was always a fearful presence, but no way of dying was more feared than death by hydrophobia. It was a horribly agonizing death, and there was no cure once a person was infected. Not until 1885 did Louis Pasteur discover the vaccine which would treat this dreaded disease. A Pasteur

Institute method for detection of this lethal virus and for treatment of its victims was not established in Texas until 1903.

Hydrophobia, or rabies, is transmitted to humans during frenzied attacks by rabid animals — mad dogs, cats, coyotes, raccoons and especially skunks. As these crazed creatures went into the final throes of their hideous torment, they would pounce insanely upon anything that moved, furiously snapping and biting and clinging until they were killed or torn away.

The incubation period for the rabies virus could range from two weeks to 60 days, thus making the victims endure the awful suspense of waiting for their inevitable and ghastly deaths. Some lucky people had a natural immunity to the disease; if they were not ill by the end of two months, they could breathe a great sign of relief, although the emotional drain of standing so long at death's door must have been nearly unbearable trauma in itself.

Most assaults by rabid animals took place during the so-called "dog days" of summer. Perhaps one all-too-familiar mad dog horror story serves as a graphic example of how terrifying these attacks could be.

In the 1880s, a family named Carter lived on a farm north of the Canadian River in northern Texas. The Carter family was six in number: a mother and father, an adolescent son, two preschool age daughters and a newly born baby.

One sultry August afternoon, while the father worked in the fields not far from the house, and the mother rocked the baby on the shady porch, the two little girls, Sissie and Olevia, scampered off to the big gate on the edge of the picket-fenced front yard. The girls loved to swing on the gate while they laughed and sang their sweet, childish songs. This day, as they swung, they heard a panting, choking sound coming from the dusty weeds on the opposite site of the road.

Moments later, a gaunt, black dog with long, soapy strings of white foam dangling from its mouth emerged and lurched toward the gate. The girls began screaming hysterically: "Mad dog! Mad dog!" Their brother, Bailey, ran at once out of the barn and shouted, "Climb the gate! Climb to the top!" As the girls scrambled up out of reach of the dog's slathering, snapping jaws, Bailey ran across the yard with his pitchfork and shinnied up the gate post. With his legs wrapped around the post and one hand clutching the top, he leaned out and tried to jab the animal with the pitchfork.

On the gate, little Sissie was shaking so badly she lost her grip and fell in front of the dog which pounced on her instantly and seized her arm. Her horrified brother stretched out as far as he possibly dared and stabbed the dog. It whirled around to fight its new opponent, giving Sissie the precious seconds she needed to reclimb the gate.

By now the children's father was running in from the fields. He dashed into the house, grabbed his shotgun and with a single blast, killed the crazed beast and rescued his family. The bitten daughter was carried, sobbing, into her home and placed on a bed. "Go get Granny Lallus," the girl's mother told her son. "Go just as fast as you can!"

Granny Lallus was something of a legend in that part of the country; she was a highly respected folk healer in a land where few accredited doctors practiced. When Granny arrived at the Carter farm, she washed Sissie's wound with a strong lye soap before she rubbed coal oil into the bite. After carefully bandaging Sissie's arm, she told Mrs. Carter, "Keep her in the house where it's cooler. Don't let her run around, and get hot. All we can do now is hope for the best."

Several days went by, and Sissie Carter showed no signs of illness. In fact, she seemed so perky and cheerful that her worried parents and brother and sister began daring to hope she might be one of the rare few who could survive a mad dog bite. Then, one morning, Sissie sat up in her bed, complaining of a severe headache. She was so thirsty she could barely talk, but when she tried to drink from the water dipper her mother pressed to her lips, she went into convulsions.

Now the Carters knew the awful truth: Sissie was doomed to die in one of the most horrible ways imaginable. All they could do was pray that her suffering would not last long. Granny Lallus joined the family in their death-bed vigil, trying to alleviate the girl's agony. Sissie begged constantly for water, but she could not swallow when it was given to her. Granny thought she might be able to drink if she could not see the water, so she blindfolded the child. But even then, Sissie could not get the water down.

When Sissie's agony finally ended, Granny Lallus drew the sheet up over the little girl's face. "Oh Lordy," she signed. "If only we'd had a madstone, we could've saved that dear child's life."

Madstones were a much sought-after folk remedy in frontier Texas. Reputedly, when one was placed on a bite wound before the rabies virus spread through the body of a victim, it would draw out the poison. Not everyone believed in the power of these stones for it did sound impossible. Still, enough tales of miraculous madstone cures have been told to give considerable credence to the survivors' claims.

Madstones were quite rare and therefore were

highly-prized. One early Texas banker, Walter Caraway of Weatherford, inherited two madstones from his grandfather. He kept one in a safe deposit box in his bank and sold the other one for one thousand dollars —a sum which in those days was equivalent to the price of a fairly sizeable ranch.

The stones themselves were small. Most could be held between a thumb and forefinger; none was larger than a goose egg. They were found in the bodies of cud-chewing, multi-stomached, horned ruminants such as cows and deer where they had formed in much the same way that pearls form in oysters or kidney stones in humans.

Since madstones developed in response to disturbances in the animal's body chemistry, it would seem reasonable that it might have medicinal qualities. And there were certainly plenty of early Texans who swore the stones' curing powers were nothing short of magical.

In 1869, a surveyor named Warren Angus Ferris, who lived near White Rock Creek on the outskirts of Dallas submitted an article to the *Dallas Herald* which he titled, "The Madstone: Is it myth or is it reality?" In what he called a "plain statement of facts," Ferris described at length his own experience with a rabid animal bite and a madstone cure.

Ferris' story began on a hot summer's night. His family had all gone off to bed, and he was enjoying a last pipeful of tobacco before retiring himself. As always in the summer, all the windows and doors had been left open. Ferris' youngest daughter, Mary Cathern, was about to doze off when a large, furry animal sprang through her bedroom window. It landed on the floor. With its claws skittering across the boards, it scrambled beneath her bed.

Mary Cathern screamed, "Daddy! There's somethin' scary under my bed! Come quick and chase it away!"

Warren Ferris hurried to his daughter's bedside, swiftly lifted her in his arms and carried her into her sister's room. After closing the door, he re-entered the darkened bedroom where he could hear the animal snarling and growling below the bed.

Ferris stamped his foot loudly. "Get outta here!" he shouted. "Go on! Shoo!" Instantly a big, wild-eyed raccoon burst out, bit Ferris on the calf of his leg and flashed away into the living room where it launched a furious attack on the rocking chair. Ferris hastily climbed out the window and groped in the dark until he found a hoe.

He cautiously snuck back inside where the maddened creature was still insanely fighting the rocker. Ferris took careful aim, swung the hoe, and stunned the raccoon enough to be able to drive it out the front door and into the yard where the family dogs finished it off, though not before both dogs had been severely bitten.

Now Ferris dropped into the rocking chair and pulled up his pantleg to examine his own wound. "Looks like it got me pretty bad," he told his frightened family as they gathered around him. "It looks deep. I'll go see a doctor first thing in the morning.

"Oh, Warren," said his wife. "There may not be much a doctor can do. What you need is a madstone."

At dawn, Warren Ferris rode off to Dallas to consult a physician. "The only thing that can be done," the doctor concluded, "is to cut out the entire bite and cauterize the wound."

Ferris winced at the thought of losing a chunk of his leg. "What about a madstone?" he asked.

"I have no faith in them myself," said the doctor. "But if you wish to try one before you submit to the operation, I understand there is a man living near Gainesville who possesses one. Unfortunately I don't know his name."

Ferris went off at once in search of the madstone. He rode north throughout the day, stopping frequently to ask the folks he met if they knew of a man who owned a madstone. At last someone said, "Oh, yes. That would be John Favens you're lookin' for. He lives out on the west fork of the Trinity River, just about three miles down yonder."

It was well after dark when Warren Ferris knocked on John Favens' door. After he had described his problem, Favens invited him in. He turned up his kerosene lamp and began rummaging through a battered, old trunk. "Here it is," he said as he laid a small, grey rock in Ferris' hand.

Ferris examined it closely. It was no more than two inches long, less than an inch thick and resembled a wasp's nest in both shape and color. The roughly-textured stone was covered with rows of extremely minute, capillary-like tubes and was as light as pumice.

Favens heated a pan of water into which he placed the stone. As soon as the madstone was wet and warm, he placed it directly on Ferris' wound. To Ferris' amazement, the stone attached itself to his leg and clung tenaciously to his skin for the next hour and a half; he could shake his leg and walk around the room without detaching it.

When at last the stone fell off, Favens put it back in the pan and brought the water to a boil. A thin, green scum promptly rose to the bubbling surface. "Yep," John Favens nodded in satisfaction. "She's drawin' poison. Y'know, I always worry about this old stone. There's some who say a madstone weakens every time it's used, and this old rock's been used a lot. Well, let's put her back on."

Favens placed the stone on the wound again and just as before, it stuck firmly. This time, less than an hour passed before the stone fell to the floor. "That's a good sign," Favens said as he boiled the green scum out of the rock.

When he tried to attach the madstone a third time, it refused to adhere to the bite. "The poison's gone," Favens smiled. "You're as good as new, Mister Ferris." Warren Ferris returned to his home a healed and healthy man while his dogs, both of which had been tied to a tree, went mad and had to be shot.

In his *Dallas Herald* article, Ferris wrote: "My theory is that the hydrophobia virus has a strong chemical affinity for one or more of the constituents of the madstone. The virus, assisted by the evaporating water and the capillary action of the tubes, ascends and combines with the constituent of the stone, forming a new compound which is soluble in hot water.

"This new compound no doubt fills the tubes and assists the ascent of the virus until washed out in hot water. Then, the stone is in a condition to be reapplied with similar result."

Madstones seemed to be capable of drawing almost any type of poison from a wound in a human body. Reputedly they were used on everything from wasp stings to rattlesnake bites. The problem with extracting the venom from the bite of a poison snake was, of course, the dire fact that snake venom travels through its victim's blood much faster than the rabies virus. A madstone had to be close at hand and be obtained as quickly as possible. Madstone cures of

A TYPICAL MADSTONE. Was it a miraculous cure or a folkloric myth?

Smithsonian Institute photo

snake bites were probably very rare on the far-flung frontier of Texas. A snake-bitten person who reached a lifesaving stone in time was a very lucky individual.

One of those fortunate few was W.F. Kahlden, who grew up on a farm in Fayette County in the 1880s. In 1881, at the age of seven, Kahlden was bitten on his bare toe by a water moccasin. He ran in a panic back to the house where his mother ordered him to lie down and calm himself. She realized that running was the worst possible thing her boy could have done since the rapid heart beat spreads the poison faster. She dashed out and called in one of the field hands. "We need the Indian's madstone right away," she told him. "Go fetch Old Clem."

Clem Knowles was an Indian whose madstone was quite famous in Fayette County. People came from far and wide to seek treatment for all kinds of infections and bites. Fortunately, Knowles' modest little cabin was within a mile of the Kahlden's so he arrived in short order.

Mrs. Kahlden had already heated a pan of water into which Knowles dropped his madstone. The bitten boy's foot and ankle were now painfully swollen, so the aged Indian gave him a stiff shot of whiskey before slitting the toe at the bite. He then placed the moistened stone on the cut. It adhered at once.

When the stone finally fell off, Knowles boiled it. As expected, dark bubbles rose in the water. He reapplied the stone several more times until it would no longer stick. A smile spread across Knowles' wrinkled face. "Your wound is clean," he told the boy. "The venom is out."

Clem Knowles graciously accepted the Kahlden family's heartfelt thanks, but, as always, he refused any payment for his services. He believed his madstone was a gift from the Great Spirit; to profit from it would be profane.

The Indian people had known of the power of madstones long before the Texans came into their land. For that matter, many other older cultures throughout the world used these healing stones to treat a variety of ailments.

The ancient Persians seem to have been the first to have somehow recognized their curative qualities. They called these mysterious rocks "padzahrs," a word meaning "expelling poison." When Europeans first began using the stones, the word became "bezoar" in English and "bezoard" in French.

Apparently bezoars were much in demand by royalty and nobility since they were often in need of antidotes for poison. It is said that Queen Elizabeth always dipped a bezoar in her wine before drinking it to guard against poison.

In today's world, madstones are all but forgotten. Nevertheless, several Texans still own madstones and still believe in the stones' remarkable powers. One such man was the late Ambrous Lee, a former chief of police in Mineral Wells. His madstone had been passed down through four generations, and he used it well into the second half of the Twentieth Century to treat people who came to his home.

Ambrous Lee had total faith in his thumb-sized, undistinguished-looking grey rock. As he often said, "If I am ever bitten by a mad dog, a rattlesnake or a poisonous spider, the only treatment I want is that little old stone placed on my wound. I know it will do the work."

Bibliography - Chapter 8

Clark, Mary Whatley. *Frontier Times*. Austin, Texas. Western Publications. February-March, 1981.

Conger, W.R. *True West*. Austin, Texas. May-June, 1966.

Dobie, J. Frank. **Madstones and Twisters.** Dallas, Texas. Southern Methodist University Press. 1940.

Forbes, Thomas R. **American Folk Medicine.** University of California. 1968.

Myers, Olevia. *True West*. Austin, Texas. Western Publications. October-November, 1963.

9

Secrets of the
Monahans Sandhills

Sand and wind are like *yin* and *yang*. Sand is *yin*, a passive and feminine element, contrasted with and complimentary to the active, masculine *yang* force of wind. Together they have defined many parts of this planet. Wind-sculpted sand dunes, awesome in their foreboding majesty and breathtaking in their delicate beauty, have challenged and charmed humanity since the earliest of times.

In Texas, the Monahans Sandhills form one of the Southwest's must interesting and unusual dune-fields. As Captain Randolph B. Marcy, commander of a U.S. Army mapping expedition, wrote in 1848: "These hills or mounds present the most singular and anomalous feature in the geology of the prairies." But in addition to being a rare geologic wonder, the sandhills have a dramatic human history as well; a dark tragedy occurred here and remains to this day as one of Texas' most perplexing, unsolved mysteries.

These great hills of sand spread out for nearly 200 miles east of the Pecos River, from the present day town of Monahans on westward and north into New Mexico. Wind began depositing sand on the harsh Texas plains more than one million years ago. Today most of the hills and dunes are stabilized by coarse, stubborn vegetation which anchors them in place with long roots.

Shinnery oaks which cover many of the slopes rarely grow taller than three feet, but can send out roots 70 feet in length. The mesquite shrub, with its fern-like leaves and long, red beans, searches for water with roots that are sometimes 175 feet long. These tenacious plants, along with sagebrush, rabbit brush and prairie yucca, have tamed most of these restless dunes and hold them firmly in their unshakable grasp.

Still, within this sprawling expanse of stabilized sand, several large "seas" of open, migratory dunes exist. Devoid of vegetation, these sweeping waves of white sand are continuously active. The wind etches them with subtle, rippling lines and sends plumes flowing lightly from their crests.

As one walks the dunes by day, there is rarely any sign of wildlife. But after the sun sets, the sand-hills come alive. In the morning, one is pleasantly startled to discover that a surprisingly large number of nocturnal animals —packrats, ground squirrels, pocket gophers, foxes and coyotes— have left their tracks on the sands. Tracks don't last long in the Monahans, however. Even human footprints can vanish in a matter of hours, brushed away by the wind's constant caretaking.

Other animals have left a more permanent record of their presence in the hills. Fossilized bones of great mammoths, giant bison, and even over-sized turtles have surfaced 10,000 years after their deaths. Among the bones of these great beasts, anthropologists have found flint projectiles, clearly indicating that these monstrous creatures had been tracked down and killed by primitive hunters.

The early paleo-Indian inhabitants of the region found the dunefield to be a suitable place to live. There was wild game to stalk and acorns, prickleypear fruit and mesquite beans to gather. Water, although scarce, was available in widely scattered ponds and seeps. And they found sheltering hummocks provided hideaways during times of danger or severe weather.

These hardy, resourceful people called the inhospitable-looking hills home for more than 5,000 years. When their time on earth inevitably passed, they were replaced by immigrants of Athabaskan stock — fierce, bold tribes who evolved into the warrior nations of the Comanches, Kiowas and Apaches. These Indians had little interest in the sandhills area. Instead, they became "the Lords of the Plains" where the great herds of buffalo roamed.

When the Spanish came to this land, they, too, ignored the sandhills. A few exploratory parties traveled through, but no missions or *presidios* were established in this region.

Later the Anglos would also find the sandhills a good place to avoid. In the 1850s, an army expedition led by Captain John Pope traversed the dunes in an attempt to determine the most feasible route for a transcontinental railroad from Texas to the Pacific coast. Pope was appalled by the barrier that he encountered.

In his diary, he wrote: "From the Pecos River to the level prairie east of the sandhills, a road passes through about 30 miles of the heaviest sand. It is the worst road anywhere. Passage is impossible for heavy-laden wagons. Even with animals perfectly fresh, and lightly loaded wagons, it requires all our exertion to overcome the difficulties of this dreadful road. Our progress is sometimes less than five miles a day."

It goes without saying that Captain Pope recommended a route that did not cross the dunes. Even so, the Texas & Pacific Railroad could not be built for several more years due to the lack of water in the area. When at last deep drilling struck groundwater beneath the dunes, construction of the railroad began. Monahans was selected as a watering stop between the Pecos River and Big Springs. The trains began to roll at last.

In the 1880s, more wells were drilled throughout the area. Windmills finally made irrigation possible. Scattered farms sprang up and produced crops of alfalfa, cotton, melons and grapes. But the interior of the great sandhills was left undeveloped and largely unexplored. The faint, faraway whistles of the passing trains were mankind's only intrusion into the lonely dunes.

One of the few men who did show an interest in this untouched, unexploitable wasteland was Colonel Arthur Hayes, a West Texas frontier judge. What drew Hayes to the dunes cannot now be determined, but in 1901 he organized a small group of like-minded, local citizens to explore the Monahans sandhills.

Hayes probably did not expect to find much on his casual expedition. He surely knew the area had no mineral potential or settlement possibilities, so presumably he simply wished to ride through a remarkable landscape which he thought no other Anglo pioneer had ever seen.

To his surprise, he soon learned his group was

definitely not the first to traverse these hills; on the party's second day out, they made a shocking discovery. Approximately six and a half miles east of the nearest road at a spot now known as Willow Springs, the riders found the charred remains of a very large wagontrain sticking out of the sand.

Hayes and his companions dismounted, scarcely able to believe what they were seeing. They walked slowly past the long rows of decaying wood and rusty iron. There were 40 wagons in all, and they had been burned. The wagontrain was laid out in a V-shaped formation... a defensive positioning often used by caravans when they camped in hostile territory.

"My God," Hayes said. "What happened here? Who were these people and what on earth were they doing out here in the middle of these dunes?" He decided then and there he would do everything he could to answer those questions.

The judge gathered up some of the relics to take back to Monahans. In the weeks that followed, he returned to the site several times to bring out more artifacts; pieces of flintlock rifles, iron yokes, wagon wheels and a few human bones.

The wagon wheels provided Hayes with his first clue to the origins of the ox-drawn train. Upon examining the wheels' rims, he found they were made of tool steel. This proved the wagontrain had come from California since tool steel was not available in the East during pioneering times, but was being sold from freight boats in San Francisco and transported on to the gold fields.

Hayes found this information very exciting; it narrowed his search down considerably. A wagontrain of this size going east when nearly every one else was heading in the opposite direction would surely have attracted quite a little attention. A search of archival records and old newspapers just might reveal who these people were, when they were passing through and where they had hoped to go.

The distance between California and the desolate, sand-blown Texas oasis where they perished is more than 1,000 miles. Their ill-fated journey would have taken them through Yuma and Tucson in the Arizona Territory, on to El Paso, and then northeast to their final campsite at Willow Springs. Their passage could not have gone unnoticed.

At his earliest opportunity, Arthur Hayes made a train trip to Yuma which had been a fort and a major resting place for caravans during the California gold rush days. Here, in the back issues of a territorial newspaper, he found a single article about the wagontrain.

According to the article, 40 wagons had arrived in Yuma in the spring of 1873. These travelers were Dutch immigrants who had worked for several years in the gold fields and now, with their families, were on their way to Missouri to buy farm lands. They had laid over in the Yuma wagonyards for several days before rolling on into obscurity.

Hayes was both elated and disappointed by the short write-up. It identified the wagontrain, but did not give any names or the numbers of its members. Unfortunately, this single scrap of information was all that he could locate. With the help of some historians from Sul Ross University, Hayes delved into archives in Tucson, El Paso and elsewhere, but found no further mention of the doomed wagons.

Nor, over the years, has anyone else. All questions regarding this tragedy remain forever unanswered. Today it can only be speculated as to what happened and to whom.

How many people were there? Since they were traveling as families, there may have been well over one hundred. Very few bones were recovered, probably because predators and vultures had carried away most of them. Thus an accurate count of skeletons was not possible; the bones were so scattered and fragmented that they eventually had to be buried in a common grave rather than as individuals.

One of the most vexing questions about the massacre is why did the wagons leave the trail and head illogically into the nearly impassible sandhills? These people were seasoned travelers. They had come to this country from the Netherlands, crossed the entire American continent to reach California, and had covered the first 1,000 miles of their return to Missouri. They were hardly the type of folks to naively wander off and get lost.

Most researchers who pondered this question concluded that the wagontrain was desperately in need of water. Since there is water at Willow Springs, a mere two feet below the surface. The paleo-Indians knew this, as did the Comanches who sporadically rode through the dunes on their way to other hunting grounds.

But Willow Springs was not the only source of water in the area. The wagoneers had to have been following a trail then known as "Lieutenant Michler's Route" which was surveyed in 1849. Maps drawn in the 1850s clearly show the locations of waterholes along this mostly arid route. There would seem to be no reason to go off-trail to seek water. And apparently, no other travelers did between 1873 and 1901, since the wagontrain was undiscovered for 28 years.

Could there be another reason for this fatal side-

trip other than a quest for water? Arthur Hayes wondered if the wagontrain was trying to hide from some
terrible threat encountered along the way. Was it too
dangerous to stay on Michler's Route? Was there something so frightening on that seldom-traveled trail that
these tough pioneers felt they needed to hide out until
the danger passed?

The Michler trail was, undeniably, a perilous
passage. Gangs of bandits, both Anglo and Mexican,
roamed West Texas in those days, attacking unwary
travelers. And the mighty Comanches raided the entire
land with near-impunity. If the caravan's detour was
an attempt to evade marauders, it was a hopeless
endeavor. The wheel ruts of 40 wagons and the hoof-
prints of the oxen and horses would have left a trail
anyone could have followed.

Whatever drew the wagontrain to Willow Springs,
whether it was water or fear, it lured them into a death
trap from which there was apparently no escape.

Who attacked these people? Bandit gangs can
probably be ruled out. The gangs were vicious, blood-
thirsty ruffians who had no qualms about committing
mass murder, but they were too small in number and
too smart to assault an entire caravan protected by at
least 40 armed and seasoned pioneers.

So if the perpetrators of the massacre were not
bandits, they may well have been Comanches. Only
this formidable tribe was powerful enough to overwhelm a wagontrain. A report issued by the U.S. Army
in 1867 estimated the Comanches had between 15,000
and 16,000 horses. They were capable of sending forth
a very large war party.

One shudders to think of the terrible battle that
would have taken place. It may have been over very
quickly, or the wagons' defenders might have held off

their attackers for quite awhile. They were fairly well positioned to withstand a siege, since they had water and undoubtedly an ample supply of food. The one thing that wouldn't have lasted long was ammunition. Once that was gone, the carnage would have begun.

On the other hand, the assault may have been sudden and swift with hundreds of painted warriors screaming into the encampment from all sides, probably just at dawn when the travelers were only half-awake. The weary night guards may have set down their rifles to pick up their first mugs of hot coffee.

However it came, the assault was furious. It was hand-to-hand combat. Hayes found several broken rifles at the site, an indication that the men were swinging them like clubs before they were cut down.

Did anyone survive the massacre? Probably all of the men were killed, but Comanches often kidnapped women and children and took them to their camps. Sometimes these captives adapted well to the harsh Indian way of life, but many died. A few escaped and some were ransomed or rescued by the U.S. Army and the Texas Rangers. But it seems that no one from the Willow Springs wagontrain was ever accounted for.

If the wagons had not been burned following the massacre, a lot more would be known about these intrepid people's journey across a savage, dangerous land. In those days, many immigrants kept diaries, carefully penned journals which recorded the details of their day-to-day progress over the frontier trails. Surely some of the pioneers who died at Willow Springs wrote diaries though they were never to be finished and never to be read.

These journals, if indeed there were any, were consumed by the fires. Their words billowed up in the smoke and were carried away by the eternal wind, the keeper of the secrets of the Monahans sandhills.

How to Visit the Monahans Sandhills

The heart of the Texas dunefield is preserved as a 3,840-acre State park six miles northeast of Monahans. To reach the park, turn off Interstate Highway 20 at exit 86 and follow Park Road 41 to the entrance station.

Monahans Sandhills State Park has both picnicking and camping facilities, as well as an extremely interesting interpretive center filled with showcases and antiques and memorabilia from the sandhills' long and unusual history. Some of the relics from the ill-fated wagontrain are now in the museum at Sul Ross State University in Alpine.

Bibliography - Chapter 9

Carson, Xanthus. *Frontier Times*. Austin, Texas. Western Publications. April-May, 1973.

Monahans Sandhills State Park. Austin, Texas. Texas Parks and Wildlife Department. July, 1989.

Texas. Austin, Texas. Texas Department of Transportation. 1992.

Thomas, Alma. **The West Texas Historical and Scientific Society Publication.** Alpine, Texas. Sul Ross State University. 1926.

Thompson, Barry B. *The Texas Permian Basin Historical Annual*. Austin, Texas. August, 1961.

10

UFOs at Night
are Big & Bright...

Deep in the heart of Texas, unidentified flying objects are far from rare. For decades, they have interrupted the tranquility of the night with their sudden appearances as they flash past the cockpits of commercial airliners, hover in backcountry skies or reveal their presence as blips on radar screens.

Texas' UFOs have been so numerous that one brief chapter cannot cover all the sightings of the past

125

50 years. However, there are several cases that are so mysterious and inexplicable that they are regarded as classics in the annals of UFOlogy.

Fascinating and sometimes frightening, these incidents deserve to be described in detail. All were reliably documented at the time they occurred. No amount of de-bunking has been able to explain them away. Taken individually or linked, they tend to prove that something very real —and possibly quite dangerous— is flying the skies and occasionally landing on the ground in this great, vast state.

The first Texas UFO flap to draw national attention took place during August and September 1951. Over a period of two weeks, flights of fast-moving, luminous aerial objects zipped over the town of Lubbock, night after night. This amazing phenomenon had an unusual beginning; the timing would prove of critical importance in the investigation that followed.

About midnight Central Standard Time on the evening of August 25, 1951, a group of Lubbock professors sitting on the porch of geologist W.I. Robinson's home saw a formation of aerial lights swoop over them. The sighting lasted only a few seconds so the men did not get a lengthy look. But they all agreed they had definitely seen something extraordinary.

Thirty minutes later, at 11:30 p.m. Mountain Standard Time, two residents of Albuquerque, New Mexico, watched spellbound as a brightly shining "wing-shaped" UFO soared over their backyard. This sighting lasted longer than the Lubbock fly-by, so the couple was able to give a detailed description of the craft later.

They said the "wing" was sharply swept back in a boomerang shape with bluish lights along its rear edge. It appeared to be much larger than a B-29 bomber and seemed to be at least 800 to 1,000 feet above the earth. The distance between Lubbock and Albuquerque is approximately 250 air-miles. To cover that distance in 30 minutes meant the object was high-balling it at 500 miles an hour.

Neither the Albuquerqueans nor the Lubbock professors were aware of each other's sightings. And they did not know one another, so they could not have colluded on their coincidental stories. Since all of them were respected members of their communities (the Albuquerque man was a high-clearance employee of the Atomic Energy Commission) the likelihood of a hoax was nil.

The Albuquerque couple reported what they had seen to an intelligence officer at Kirtland Air Force Base. The officer interviewed them, accepted a drawing of the object, and sent the information off to Project Blue Book, the Air Force's official investigative probe of UFOs.

Due to public criticism of the Air Force's efforts in researching earlier UFO sightings, Project Blue Book had been newly reorganized, was well-staffed and funded, and was making serious attempts at thorough investigations.

In Lubbock, the professors also told the Air Force about their sighting. Then they decided to do a bit of sky-watching. Each night from their separate porches and patios, they craned their necks and scanned the skies. Their vigils paid off immediately. On the night of August 26, the elderly gentlemen again witnessed flights of overhead lights, twice within a couple of hours.

Now W.I. Robinson went to the local newspaper. When his amazing story was published, scores of Lubbock citizens took up sky-watching. Dozens of "Lubbock lights" were excitedly reported: single lights, pairs, and of course, great, awesome formations of lights. No one doubted that the phenomena were real, but they remained unexplainable.

One night in early September, a local game warden spotted a couple of the lights. As they passed by, one of them made a soft sound, a sort of "chur-wee." noise. The warden laughed out loud; he was instantly sure he had solved the mystery of the "Lubbock Lights." The whistling notes he had heard were the cries of a plover.

Plovers are common grassland birds in Texas. Spritely and swift, they constantly flit about in search of insects. Their breasts and the undersides of their wings are a dull white. Plovers have always been so familiar to Texans that they pretty much ignore them. Now the game warden believed the citizens of Lubbock were suddenly paying special attention to the plovers because they were literally seeing them in an entirely different light.

In one section of town, the old-fashioned street lights had recently been replaced by new, modern mercury vapor lights. When the plovers darted past these lights snaring insects, their white feathers briefly but startlingly reflected the glow, creating a flashing, momentary illusion of an unidentified flying object.

A lot of people accepted the warden's theory, especially those folks who had seen only single lights or no lights at all. Those who had seen the lights in formation were, to say the least, somewhat skeptical of this simple explanation. First of all, plovers do not "flock." They appear in pairs or in threesomes, but never in V-shaped flightlines like geese or cranes. And they do not cross the sky from horizon to horizon in a matter of seconds.

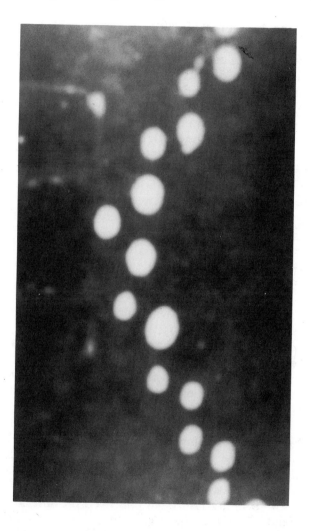

LUBBOCK LIGHTS photograph by Carl Hart. Those who attempted to prove it a fraud could not duplicate the effects the amateur photographer caught on film.

The Air Force officials, eager to find a natural explanation for the lights, were more than happy to accept the birds as the answer. This explanation would probably have gone into Project Blue Book's files had it not been for an amateur, teenaged photographer, Carl R. Hart, Jr. On the evening of August 31, 1951, Hart photographed not one, but two, flights of Lubbock Lights. And they did not look like plover bellies at all.

August 31 was a hot night in Lubbock. Hart had pushed his bed close to the window in hopes of catching a breeze. As he gazed out at the sky, a spectacular display of lights streaked by. Having heard that one flight was often followed by another, Carl Hart grabbed his camera and hurried outdoors. He opened the lens as far as it would go, to f3.5. Then he set the shutter at one 60th of a second, which was the slowest speed he thought he could hand-hold. Finally he sprawled out on the grass to wait.

He did not have to wait long. Soon a great curving line of 19 lights soared across the night. Hart jumped up in time to snap two pictures. He had no sooner settled back down when another cluster of glowing, circular objects flew over. Hart clicked his camera three times before the lights disappeared in the distance.

The next morning, he went at once to the home of a friend who had a darkroom. Hart fully expected to be disappointed by his attempts to take pictures in the middle of the night, but when the film was developed he was absolutely astounded. The photos were fantastic.

All 19 lights had been captured on film, shining like bright holes in the night sky. They were aligned in a sharp bow, and nearly all the lights were in pairs. Could it be that this youthful, non-professional photographer had actually taken pictures of the tail lights of a UFO?

Hart took his pictures to the local newspaper, but the editor declined to run them until he could assign one of his own photographers to attempt a duplication of the amateur's work. That night, a professional newspaper photographer went "plover hunting" in Lubbock. Several times during the course of the evening, illuminated birds did fly past the vapor lights as the newspaperman clicked away. But even though he was using super-fast film and lengthy time exposures, none of the birds showed up in his photographs after development. The images were simply too dim. The vapor lights themselves did appear, of course, but they were easily identifiable. The street lights could not, at any location in town, be lined up in the arching pattern shown in Hart's photos.

The editor called Carl Hart the next morning to say, "Kid, I don't know what the hell you took pictures of, but they're gonna be on the front page tomorrow."

Within hours after the newspaper hit the streets, two Air Force intelligence officers knocked on Hart's door to ask permission to borrow the negatives so they could be examined at Wright-Patterson Air Force Base's photo interpretation laboratory. Hart consented. His pictures were put through a series of tests which revealed no signs of fakery. But neither did they yield any explanation of what the lights in the negative might be.

Copies of Carl Hart's photographs wound up in Project Blue Book's files under the label "unidentified." The Lubbock lights continued to appear throughout early September. Then , as quickly as it began, the flap ended. The plovers and the vapor lights were still in town, but the Lubbock lights were not.

What had they been? And where had they come

from? Perhaps part of the answer came out of the sky a little over a year later when a spectacular, radar-confirmed sighting was reported near Galveston.

Late on the night of December 6, 1952, Air Force Captain John Harter was piloting a B-29 on a night practice flight over the Gulf of Mexico. The plane was about 200 miles from Galveston when the radar officer, Lieutenant Sid Coleman, saw an unidentified blip appear on his screen. "Captain, I'm picking up something strange," Coleman said in a strained voice. "I've got an 'unknown' here and it's traveling 13 miles with each sweep. Sergeant Bailey and I calculate that to be 5,000 miles an hour!"

"Ah, c'mon, Sid," the captain scoffed. "Nothing in the world travels that fast. You've got a malfunction. Recalibrate your set."

"It's no malfunction, captain," conformed the plane's navigator, Lieutenant Cassidy. "I'm showing the same blip on my screen, at the same speed. Wow! There's another one! No, make that three more! We're picking up four 'unknowns.'"

"And I'm picking up four *visuals*," Captain Harter gasped. "I can see them! Twelve o'clock high, heading right for us!"

Within moments, the awe-struck crew held their breath as four brilliant, bluish white objects shot by their aircraft. The objects were so close and so bright that the interior of the plane lit up during the split-second it took the UFOs to pass. Harter slumped in his seat and rubbed his brow with nervous hands. "Whew. That was too close for comfort."

Lieutenant Cassidy returned his attention to his radar screen. "Uh-oh," he said. "I don't think we're rid of them yet, captain. They've reversed their direction. They're coming back, and they're slowing down."

It was a matter of seconds before the UFOs caught up with the B-29. They reduced their speed to match that of the plane, and paced it for nearly half a minute before accelerating out of sight.

As Coleman and Cassidy watched their radar screens, a fifth "unknown" suddenly appeared. It created an enormous blip also traveling at 5,000 miles per hour. Then the radar officers stared in disbelief as something totally unbelievable happened, One by one, the smaller blips merged with the larger one.

"Good God!" Coleman hollered. "That's a mother ship! The others have boarded it!" Once all the small blips disappeared, the giant "unknown" vanished from the B-29's radar screens at a speed of *9,000* miles an hour.

When Captain Harter landed his plane in Galveston, the crew that swung down from the aircraft must have been psyched up like men returning from a combat mission. As calmly as possible, they told their superior officers about their encounter. When they were questioned individually, their stories matched in every detail. The plane's radar sets were found to be in perfect working condition. The report of the incident eventually made its way into Project Blue Book's growing list of "unidentified" cases.

Weird as this episode was, there were even stranger things yet to appear in the Texas night.

In the corner of the state, 31 miles from Lubbock, lies a small, cotton-country town called Levelland. The town's name is appropriate since it is surrounded by the flat, featureless West Texas plains. Levelland is a quiet little place where nothing much out of the ordinary ever happens. Surely none of the good folks living there ever dreamed their hometown would become famous for being the scene of one of the most intensive UFO controversies of all times.

The tale of the "Levelland Landings" began November 3, 1957. At 10:30 p.m., Hockley County Deputy Sheriff A.J. Fowler received a phone call from a very excited farm worker, Pedro Saucedo. "Mister Fowler!" Saucedo blurted out. "Me'n Joe Salaz just seen a flying saucer!"

"Sure you did," the deputy chuckled good naturedly. "What is this? Some kinda joke?"

"Its no joke, man. This thing was real! I was driving my truck west on 116 about four miles from town when Joe and me both seen this really bright light out in a field. And then it rose up, changed from blue to red, and headed right at us! My engine died, and the headlights went out. It was comin' in so low I thought it was gonna hit the truck, so I dived out and rolled across the road. Old Joe was so scared he couldn't even move. He just sat there and watched it zoomin' in.

"When that thing went over it was like a windstorm with thunder. It rocked my truck back and forth. And the heat! Man, was it hot! Then it just zipped up and was gone."

"Pedro, have you and Joe been drinking?" Fowler asked in an irritated voice. "I think you boys better go home and sleep it off. You'll be seeing pink elephants next." He plunked down the phone. But 15 minutes later it rang again.

This time the caller was a farmer named Jim Wheeler who also reported seeing a UFO while driving. Wheeler's story was almost identical to Saucedo's except it occurred east of town rather than west. The farmer said he had encountered a glaringly bright, 200-foot long, red, "egg-shaped" object sitting on the road. As he approached it, his car's engine conked out and the headlights shut off. The UFO sat silently in front of him for a few minutes before suddenly shooting straight up and away. Wheeler restarted his car and drove at once to the nearest pay phone. Fowler's next call came from José Alvarez, who jabbered excitedly about a big, red, egg-shaped aerial object that killed the engine of his pickup. Now the deputy began taking the calls seriously. He told the sheriff: "Weir, there's something crazy going on out there tonight. Everybody's seeing UFOs!"

Just then, a truck driver named James Long dashed into the office shouting, "You won't believe what I just saw!"

"Let me guess... a giant, flying egg, right?" the deputy said as his phone started to ring again.

Sheriff Weir Clem and Deputy Patrick McCullogh drove outside of town on Highway 116 where they, along with two state policemen and Levelland's constable, witnessed a brightly lighted aerial object above a field. Throughout the course of the night, eight people reported sightings to the sheriff's office along with an equal number who called the state highway patrol and the local police station.

When the Air Force heard about the rash of sightings, they were quick to discredit the eyewitness accounts. The military issued a press release which called the sightings "exaggerations or misinterpretations of natural phenomena." The statement noted that there had been thunderstorms in the area earlier, so everyone was just seeing rare displays of ball lighting. The motorists, in their excitement, had accidentally killed the engines of their cars themselves.

In spite of the hasty official explanation, reports

continued to pour into Levelland nightly for nearly a week. All had a common storyline: brilliant, shining objects appeared unexpectedly, either in the air or on the ground, and the observers' car motors died. Their headlights went out and their car radios faded. As soon as the objects abruptly swooped away, the vehicles were easily restarted.

One of the most interesting cases was a multiple witness encounter on November 5. James Stokes, who later described his experience to the police, said he was driving toward El Paso when his car engine stalled. As he coasted onto the shoulder, he noticed several people standing by their cars, staring and pointing at a large, red, oval-shaped object flying toward the road.

The light buzzed the parked cars, swung around in a wide circle and made a second pass. Each time it went over, Stokes felt intense heat. Soon after the UFO disappeared, his face, hands and wrists began to itch and redden as if they were sunburned. No one was able to convince James Stokes that all he had seen was a flash of ball lightning.

After the wave of "Levelland Landings" subsided, UFO sightings in Texas became sporadic again for nearly a decade. Then a rather disturbing close encounter took place in 1967. This perplexing incident —if it actually happened— was frightening since it indicated some sort of communication was taking place between an earthbound terrestrial vehicle and a UFO.

At three in the morning of June 24, 1967, Ray Rosi was returning from a night of fishing at Lake Travis near Austin. As he drove the nearly deserted road between Mansfield Dam and the city, a small, red sports car with two male occupants pulled up behind him. The car followed Rosi for a few miles before swinging around to pass. After the sports car sped out of sight, Rosi drove over a rise in the land from which he saw a great, bluish light hovering above the horizon. The red car had parked on the edge of the road and was flashing its headlights on and off at the aerial object.

Astonished and curious, Rosi also stopped. Apparently this disturbed the men in the sports car, since they quickly drove over a hill out of Rosi's line of vision. Soon the hovering light began to move forward. As it came nearer, Rosi could see it was a very large, cigar-shaped craft. Impulsively he jumped from his car, flashlight in hand. He began blinking a flickering barrage of random signals. First he blinked out an S.O.S., then the mathematical number for pi, and then "shave and a haircut, two bits."

To his amazement, the giant spaceship paused and its brightness diminished. Later Rosi would say, "I felt like I was being watched... like I was a kid out in the backyard doing something I shouldn't while an adult in the house was watching me. Yet there was also a feeling of communication, as if someone was trying to reach me through mental telepathy, sending a message beyond my ability to receive."

The UFO remained stationary only for a moment. Then it disappeared into a low cloud bank moving in from the south.

Later in the day, Ray discussed his experience with an Air Force intelligence officer and filled out the standard forms which were eventually stamped "insufficient data for scientific analysis" by Project Blue Book. Rosi was never able to convince any authorities that his encounter was real.

Actually, Rosi may have been very lucky that all he suffered was frustration. Others who have been that close to a UFO have not been so fortunate. A similar

incident that occurred in 1980 had a horrifying aftermath which forever ruined the lives of the witnesses.

The incredible event took place at approximately
9 p.m. on December 29. Betty Cash, Vickie Landrum
and seven year old Colby Landrum, all of Dayton, were
driving home from Houston. The road to Dayton is
tree-lined, rural and lonely at night. As the trio's car
curved around a bend, they suddenly confronted a
huge, diamond-shaped aerial object hovering above the
road. The UFO seemed to be in trouble; it was spewing
out a great jet of flame, making a roaring noise along
with a shrill beeping sound.

Fearing they would be killed if they stayed in the
car, all the people got out. Young Colby was even more
terrified outside the car, so within less than a minute
he scrambled back in. Vickie Landrum remained out of
the automobile for three to five minutes while Betty
Cash got back in after seven to ten minutes.

By now the car's interior was almost unbearably
hot, so Cash turned on the air conditioning. The UFO,
still belching fire and seemingly fighting to stay aloft,
began drifting away. Then, incredibly, a flight of 23
helicopters arrived on the scene and "escorted" the
craft out of sight. Cash and the Landrums quickly
drove to their homes in Dayton.

Then, within days, the horror began.

Colby Landrum's eyes became swollen and
watery; his skin reddened and he complained of stomach pain and diarrhea. Vickie Landrum and Betty Cash
also suffered these same ailments, but also they began
losing their hair. Later when it grew back, it was thinner, drier and grey.

Worse yet, all three of them found their eyesight
impaired. Colby, whose vision had been perfect, now
needed glasses. Betty's vision also diminished. Vickie

developed a cataract in her left eye and a glaucoma-like tunnel vision in the right.

A radiologist who examined the three victims concluded, "There is strong evidence that the symptoms were caused by ionizing radiation plus ultraviolet and infrared radiation. The nausea, the hair falling out, the blisters, the low blood count... it's just like the survivors of Hiroshima and Nagasaki."

The Cash/Landrum case drew the attention of UFOlogists from across the country. Representatives from the Mutual UFO Network (MUFON), the Aerial Phenomena Research Organization (APRO), and the Center for UFO Studies (CUFOS) all converged on little Dayton, Texas. They managed to find several eyewitnesses who had also seen the helicopters although apparently no one other than Cash and the Landrums had seen the diamond-shaped craft. The helicopters were identified as being mostly CH-47s, commonly known as "Chinooks" or "flying bananas," while others were smaller, single-rotored UH-1 "Hueys."

The military steadfastly denied it had any helicopters flying that night. Even the Army Inspector General could find no evidence to the contrary.

As time went on the three victims' physical conditions continued to worsen. Both of the Landrums broke out in sores which permanently scarred their faces and arms. In 1982, Betty Cash suffered a heart attack as well as a stroke that left her temporarily paralyzed. The women attempted to sue the government for damages, but, with the military continuing to insist it had no such aircraft as the UFO described by Cash and Landrum, the suit went nowhere.

Just what was the terrifying, flame-spouting flying diamond near Dayton that night? If the Air Force was lying, the UFO could have been a top secret, experimental aircraft of some sort. When the craft began experiencing difficulties and appeared ready to crash, the military may have dispatched helicopter teams to seal off the crash site. If the vehicle did go down, it must have been in a very remote area. Or perhaps it managed to reach Fort Hood or White Sands Missile Range.

On the other hand, if the Air Force is telling the truth and does not have any such experimental aircraft, the only other explanation would seem to be that the UFO was of extraterrestrial origin. The helicopters could be explained in one of two ways. They may have actually been Chinooks and Hueys sent by the military to track and monitor the spaceship. Or they were actually UFOs themselves designed to look like military aircraft.

The mystery of the Dayton UFO will very likely remain unsolved. Like so many other great Texas mysteries, it will remain a tantalizing enigma.

Bibliography - Chapter 10

Adams, Thomas R. **The Choppers —And the Choppers.** Paris, Texas. Project Stigmata. 1991.

Randle, Kevin D. **The UFO Casebook**. New York. Warner Books, Inc. 1989.

Schuessler, John. *Mutual UFO Network Journal.* Sequin, Texas. November, 1981.

Spencer, John. **World Atlas of UFOs.** New York. Smithmark Publishers, Inc. 1991.

Story, Ronald D. **The Encyclopedia of UFOs.** New York. Dolphin Books. 1980.

Teich, Mark. *Omni* magazine. New York. Omni Publications. February, 1983.

11
Santa Ana's Lost Payroll

He was called "The Napoleon of the West." He was a brilliant strategist in the classic tradition of the chess-like battles of his time, and a master of the political intrigues which accompanied these enormous power plays. Revered by his army, praised by his church and cheered by the ragged masses who supported him, he rode haughtily through Mexico's most tumultuous era.

His full name was Antonio López de Santa Ana Pérez de Lebrón. Born in the mountains of Jalapa to a lower elite family in 1795, Santa Ana enrolled as a youth in a royal Spanish regiment. He must have lied about his age, for he was only 15 when the Revolution of 1810 began. Apparently he served well in that bloody affair, as he received a decoration for bravery and a full lieutenancy.

Santa Ana could see that Spain was destined to lose eventually, so he switched sides and served under General Joaquín de Arredondo as a captain. When

Mexico became independent, President Vicente Guer-rero gave Santa Ana command of a full division.

Spain made one final attempt to reconquer Mexi-co in 1829, but General Santa Ana's highly disciplined troops defeated the Spanish landings at Tampico, mak-ing the general a national hero.

Santa Ana was not a modest man; he relished his fame and styled himself accordingly. His uniform was resplendent at all times with its tall, stiff collar and epaulets the size of hairbrushes. Around his waist he wore a scarlet sash above his gleaming sabre. One can assume that anyone going into battle in such a flashy outfit cared considerably more about his appearance than his personal safety.

The army Santa Ana commanded stretched out for miles. His officers, like himself, rode fine, thorough-bred steeds while the infantry, always numbering in the thousands, marched in perfect cadence with their collars buttoned and their bayoneted muskets on their shoulders. Behind them came the batteries of cannons and two giant siege guns, followed by supply trains carrying all the essential material for conducting long, hard military campaigns.

Included in the creaking wagons' cargoes of food and ammunition, blankets and bandages was the army's payroll: many sturdy, wooden chests filled with silver pesos. Santa Ana always paid his men at the end of a victorious campaign, for he knew his troops would fight harder knowing they would be financially reward-ed if they won. And, of course, Santa Ana also knew there would be a lot fewer men on his payroll at the end of a war.

By 1835, trouble was brewing between Texas and Mexico. Although the majority of settlers were loyal to Mexico, a growing, militant faction was calling for

Texas' independence. From Matamoros, Santa Ana's brother-in-law, General Martín Perfecto de Cós, issued a very firm statement: all Texans were citizens of Mexico who must submit to the government of Mexico, and continue to adhere to the Mexican Constitution as they had originally agreed to do.

Steven Austin, founder of the first American colony in Mexico's Texas, gave up his dream of maintaining a non-combative, pluralistic commonwealth under the Mexican flag. He joined the rebels in their demand for the "Americanization of Texas." A call-to-arms spread across the land, and colonists rallied in droves. Mexican troops crossed the Rio Grande and the war began.

Santa Ana, who was now president of Mexico as well as commander of the army, decreed that all Anglo-Texans were to be driven out of Texas into exile. Never again would any North Americans be permitted to settle in Texas. At the head of his 7,000-man army, Antonio López Santa Ana began his sweep across Texas in January of 1836.

It was the biggest mistake of his life.

Santa Ana made a forced march to San Antonio, moving his troops faster than any Texan believed possible. Once he had set up a headquarters in that town, the general dispatched 4,000 of his troops to attack a small, nearby barrier fort which guarded the southern flank of Anglo-Texas —a walled former Spanish mission called the Alamo.

Surely every American and Mexican citizen has heard the story of the Alamo. It is one of the more legendary battles in the history of either nation. The story has been told and re-told how 150 American frontiersmen held off an army of 4,000 for 13 days from behind the cannon-battered ramparts of this cold, stone fortress.

Mexican ballads have extolled the courage of the Mexican solders who marched in formation unflinch-ingly through the withering gunfire from above, carry-ing assault ladders, trying in vain to scale the walls. American folk songs have praised the valor of the men who defended those walls with a willingness to die to the last man for "God and Texas. Victory or Death."

When it was over, Santa Ana had lost 1,600 of his finest, bravest soldiers and every one of the 150 defenders was dead. The general, who had prudently waited out the battle in his headquarters in San Anto-nio, had paid a terrible price for his victory. But now only a small, rag-tag army commanded by Sam Hous-ton stood between him and the Brazos River.

Houston's troops were badly outnumbered, and most were untrained volunteers who knew how to shoot and fight as rugged individuals, but knew noth-ing of the formal Napoleonic tactics used so effectively by Santa Ana. The Texas general knew his undisci-plined men would be decimated in any battle fought on open ground of Santa Ana's choosing. Houston needed time to train and recruit, but time was running out fast. He began a series of strategic withdrawals.

Gloating over Houston's weakness, Santa Ana split his forces into separate columns which raged across the land burning towns and farms and driving hundreds of terrified refugees ahead of them. The Mex-ican general was so overly confident that he decided to personally lead the column that would deal the death blow to Houston's contemptible excuse for an army.

He pressed relentlessly forward as Houston retreated and retreated again. Houston's men were grumbling; many of them deserted in disgust. But the American general knew exactly what he was doing: he was luring Santa Ana into a trap, to a place where he could fight on a battlefield of his own choice.

Sam Houston reached the banks of the San Jacinto River and the edge of Buffalo Bayou on April 18, 1836. Here, beyond a ground swell on an open prairie, he positioned his 918-man army.

Santa Ana arrived on the 20th and set up his camp on the opposite side of the swell, three-quarters of a mile away from the Texans. He ordered a brush barricade built in front of his troops and sat back to wait for his reinforcements. General Cós and 400 soldiers joined him on the morning of April 21. This brought the Mexican troop strength to 1,300, more than enough to overwhelm Houston's small, semi-civilian army.

The *comandante* gave his troops the afternoon off, to rest, take *siestas* and be fresh for the assault he planned to launch in the morning. Incredibly, he posted no sentries.

This was the moment Houston had been waiting for. He lined his foot soldiers in long rows behind the earthen mound, poised his horse-mounted troops on both flanks, and ordered 30 men to push and tow his two cannons on the top of the rise in the grassy prairie. Seated on his magnificent horse, Saracen, General Houston drew his sword. "Hold your fire until you can make it count," he shouted. "Forward... Texas!"

With that, his lines of soldiers who barely knew how to march surged forth. They were within 100 yards of the Mexican camp before they were sighted. The frantic bugle call of *centinela alerto* was drowned out by the roar of the cannons, known as the Twin Sisters, which blew enormous holes in the flimsy, make-shift barricades Santa Ana's men had piled up. Through these holes, the Texans charged, bellowing and shooting at the totally surprised Mexican soldiers. Some managed to return the fire, but most were gunned down without rifles in their hands.

Panic reigned. Some of Santa Ana's troops plunged into the treacherous Buffalo Bayou and drowned. Those who fled across the open grasslands were mercilessly chopped down by sword-swinging cavalrymen. The battle of San Jacinto lasted a mere 18 minutes. When the smoke and the screams died away, 630 Mexican soldiers were dead, 700 had surrendered, and Santa Ana was a prisoner of war. The Texans suffered two dead and 24 wounded... one of those was General Houston whose foot was shattered by a musket ball which also killed his beloved Saracen.

Houston propped himself up against the trunk of a tree with his blood-filled boot stretched out before him as he received the reports coming in from the shambles of the battlefield.

Amid the debris, the main item of value turned out to be a single oaken chest filled with silver Mexican pesos. Later, when the coins were counted, they totalled the equivalent of 11,000 American dollars. It was obviously part of Santa Ana's payroll, but where was the rest of it?

Santa Ana's army was originally 7,000 men. No doubt they earned pitifully low wages, but $11,000 would have averaged less than $2 per soldier for a campaign of several months' duration. There had to have been a lot more silver in Santa Ana's supply train.

Some historians have estimated that there should have been at least 24 such paychests. What happened to them? It would have been utterly impossible for the chests to have been buried during the frenzied 18-minute battle, so there was speculation that the chests might have been dragged to the banks of the bayou and tossed in. This seems highly unlikely since the panic-stricken Mexican soldiers were thinking only of saving their lives, not their back pay.

It is possible that when Santa Ana split his army into five separate divisions, he also divided up the pay-chests. Generals Urrea, Filisola, Ramirez y Sesma, Amat and Cós might well have been transporting size-able amounts of bright, silver coins as they advanced across the land.

After San Jacinto, when the defeated Santa Ana was forced by General Houston to issue orders for the "retirement" of the rest of his army, there would have been plenty of time for these distant units to bury their strongboxes. However, if Santa Ana did divide the pay-roll amongst his columns, General Cós would have been carrying his share when he arrived to reinforce his commander, but no paychests were found in his supply train.

Another possibility exists. Perhaps all of the money was at San Jacinto after all. Maybe, as Houston's men rummaged through the wagons, some of them stumbled upon the paychests. It would not be surprising if the finders decided to be keepers. Without much effort, they could have carried the chests under cover of darkness out onto the grasslands and buried them or taken them to the banks of the bayou and submerged them. Maybe the one chest that was found "officially" had been overlooked by the looters.

Sam Houston's men were nearly all farmers and colonists who knew that they would be returning to farms and towns burned to the ground by Santa Ana's ruthless eradication. Who can blame them if they felt Santa Ana's soldiers should foot the bill for the neces-sary rebuilding?

The contents of the single chest were evenly

divided amongst all of Houston's men: approximately $12 apiece. Additionally, each man was given a credit of $16 on his back pay which he could use to bid in an auction of Santa Ana's equipment, horses and saddles. Shortly thereafter, General Houston's victorious army, enriched and exuberant, left the battlefield to return to their families.

Did some of them return later to recover the treasure they had hidden away? If the silver was buried somewhere on the grassy prairie, it would not be difficult to dig up. But if it was sunk in the marshy bayou, it might well have been impossible to retrieve.

Over the years, a lot of people have come to believe there is a treasure hidden somewhere on the San Jacinto battlefield. In 1969, a private group of treasure hunters using magnetometers determined there was something metallic deep in the bog. They applied to the State government for a permit to do an excavation, but the Texas Antiquities Commission ruled against their request, since it would desecrate this highly-revered piece of land.

So, the treasure, if it exists, remains a part of the San Jacinto Battleground State Historic Site, hidden forever beneath the surface of this legend-shrouded place where the history of Texas was changed for all time.

How to Visit the San Jacinto Battleground

The San Jacinto Battleground State Historical Site is located in La Porte east of downtown Houston off Highway 225 on Highway 134. The site is dominated by a great white tower rising 570 feet above the flat coastal plain. One can only speculate whether or not a sizeable treasure lies beneath these venerated grounds.

Bibliography - Chapter 11

Crawford, Ann F. **The Eagle: The Biography of Santa Anna.** Austin, Texas. University of Texas. 1967.

Fehrenbach, T.R. **Lone Star: A History of Texas and the Texans.** New York. Wings Books. 1968.

Green, Ford. *Old West.* Austin, Texas. Western Publications, Inc. November-December, 1974.

Santos, **Richard G. Santa Anna's Campaign Against Texas, 1835-1836.** Austin, Texas. University of Texas. 1968.

12

One Arm, a Six Gun & a Badge

Of all the bold and reckless men who thundered across the western frontier, none gained greater legendary status than the gunfighters... men like Billy the Kid and Pat Garrett, Wyatt Earp and Doc Holliday became the West's most romanticized folk heroes. From Dodge City to Deadwood, from Lincoln County to Tombstone, the gunslingers blazed their way to immortality.

And yet, even though these never-to-be-forgotten heroes and villains were deadly men, and the violence they inflicted upon one another was spectacularly dramatic, the bloody exploits of their Texas counterparts were even more awesome. The great gunfighters of Texas were meaner and colder, quicker and bolder than all the rest. But oddly enough, they have received less national recognition and their epic battles are poorly remembered.

One Texas gunfight in particular was so wild it may well have been the ultimate shoot-out in the history of the West. It took place in 1889, and its sheer ferocity makes the famous gunfight at the OK Corral seem like a small-time skirmish in comparison. The inquests, indictments and trials that followed this savage affair left many questions forever unanswered; there has never been agreement on why things happened the way they did that fateful day.

The events which led up to this monumental fight had their beginnings in what is now Oklahoma, but which was at that time called "the Indian Territory." It was also known as "Badman's Territory," since, due to the complexities of the territory's laws, it had become a haven for outlaws of all types.

In the Indian Territory, no state law officers could legally arrest wanted criminals, and Indian police officers were not empowered to arrest outlaws for crimes committed outside their reservations. Even U.S. marshals had no authority to make arrests in the territory without a federal warrant.

It was, therefore, quite a simple matter for gangs of bandits to rob banks and steal horses in Texas and then gallop off to the relative safety of Badman's Territory. One of the worst and most feared of these gangs was a ruthless, outrageously brazen pack of horse thieves known as the Marlow Boys.

The Marlows plundered the ranches of north Texas as if they owned them. They took what they wanted and anyone who tried to stand up to them either backed down or died.

The Marlow Boys were brothers, five of them in all. Charlie was the oldest; George was two years younger, and Alf and Lep (short for Alferd and Lewellen) were twins. All of the brothers were extremely mean, but the youngest, Boone, was downright vicious. By 1888, he had already killed more than once and was soon to kill again.

The lawman destined to go up against this fanatical bunch was as highly respected as the Marlows were despised. His name was Edward W. Johnson. In March of 1885, Johnson had been appointed a U.S. marshal and was assigned to Graham, Texas, since Graham was at that time the last U.S. Court north and west of Dallas.

Johnson was a dedicated and courageous officer of the law; he was fast and accurate with a pistol. Although he preferred to avoid gunplay whenever possible, he never hesitated to engage in it when someone resisted arrest. Marshal Johnson quickly earned a formidable reputation as an uncompromising lawman.

Then in 1887 in Wichita Falls, he attempted to arrest an outlaw named Bob James. James drew his gun and Johnson shot and killed him, but not before James managed to get off a shot that hit Johnson in the right arm.

The marshal's arm was so badly shattered it had to be amputated. This, everyone thought, would put an end to Johnson's career as a law officer, but they underestimated this stalwart man's determination. Ed Johnson simply switched his holster to his left hip and began practicing drawing and firing with his left hand. Within a surprisingly short time, he became just as swift and accurate as he had been before.

Johnson's first public display of his newly acquired prowess came one afternoon after the marshal and the local sheriff, Marion Wallace, had been tipping a few at one of Graham's saloons. Johnson boasted he could place four dimes on a tree trunk, step back ten paces, turn and fire and hit at least three dimes out of four every time.

When Wallace scoffed, Johnson said, "I'm willin' to demonstrate it for you if you'd like."

Immediately, Wallace, Johnson and all the saloon's other patrons trooped out into the street headed for the edge of town. There, Marion Wallace began carefully balancing four dimes at various places on the bark of a large tree.

"Hold it, Marion," Johnson said. "I want them placed in a row."

Wallace scowled. "You didn't say nothin' about puttin' 'em in a row. What is this, some kinda trick?"

"It's no trick," Johnson declared. "And I resent your sayin' it is."

"Well, I'm the sheriff of this here county, and I got the right to set the rules for this here contest!" Wallace thundered.

The two men began arguing heatedly, shouting profanity at one another. Wallace, who was a very hot-headed man, grew so angry he went for his gun. In a lighting-fast move, Johnson drew his pistol and leveled it on Wallace before the sheriff's gun was half-way out of its holster. "Don't even think about tryin' it," the marshal said coldly. The chagrined sheriff let his pistol drop back in the holster.

"Now then," Johnson continued. "Since it seems to mean so much to you, Marion, I'll shoot the dimes the way you placed them." His gun roared four times and three perforated coins spun to the ground. From that day on, no one doubted this one-armed man's ability to perform his job as a U.S. marshal.

In the late spring of 1888, during a raid on a Texas ranch, Boone Marlow shot and killed a cowhand named Jim Halstein. A federal grand jury indicted Boone for murder. A federal warrant for his arrest was handed to Marshal Johnson. This was the chance Johnson had been waiting for.

"I'm not only goin' to bring Boone in," he told his deputies, "I'm goin' to bring in the whole damn bunch. We'll have to bend the law a little because we have no warrants for the other four. But once we get 'em out of the territory and onto Texas soil, they can be legally arrested on state charges for horse stealin'."

Johnson rounded up a six-man posse consisting of two deputy marshals, Sheriff Wallace and two of his deputies. Once the posse crossed the Red River into the Indian Territory, they were joined by two Indian Lighthorse Police officers. The Indians knew exactly where to go.

"Those Marlow Boys have a big farm where they live with their wives and their mother," the Indians informed Johnson. "They will not know we are coming. We can make an ambush on them."

"Let's ride," the marshal said.

Two days later, the heavily armed posse carefully approached the Marlows' farm. Beyond the houses and barns, they saw four unarmed men working in the fields. At a gallop, the posse swooped down on the men and at rifle point, placed them under arrest. They were Charlie, George, Alf and Lep Marlow. "You ain't got no right to do this, marshal," Charlie growled.

"I'm doin' it though, ain't I?" Johnson replied. "Where's Boone?"

"He ain't here," Charlie said with a smirk. "And it's a damn good thing for you he ain't."

Once the prisoners were securely handcuffed and shackled, the lawmen cautiously searched the houses and barns as the Marlow women glared sullenly at them. When the posse was satisfied that Boone definitely was not on the property, they confiscated an enormous arsenal of firearms, buffalo guns, shotguns, assorted rifles and .45 caliber six-shooters, all of the best makes and with plenty of ammunition.

"That ain't even half the weapons we got," George Marlow sneered. "Boone knows where the rest are, and when he comes back and finds out what you done here today, he's gonna come after you, marshal."

"I'll be lookin' forward to it," Johnson said.

The posse loaded the Marlow Boys in a wagon and headed back for Texas. They constantly watched the trail behind them as well as the trail ahead. At night, they built no campfires and posted guards around their campsite. At the end of the third day, they crossed the Red River back into Texas without incident. Boone had not struck, and most of the officers breathed a sigh of relief. Ed Johnson, however, was visibly disappointed. He gazed back across the river and said, "Next time, Boone."

The prisoners were soon lodged in the Young County jail in Graham to await trial. Security at the jail was rather lax, perhaps due to the model prisoners, docile and well-behaved. Then early one morning, Deputy Sheriff "Dink" Allen entered the jailhouse to discover two bars had been sawed out of a window and all of the Marlows were gone.

It was never determined who slipped them the saw, but apparently the hated Marlow Boys had at least one friend or accomplice in Young County.

Marshal Johnson had little difficulty in recapturing the escapees since they were unarmed and on foot. Within 24 hours, he locked them up for the second time.

Earlier, bond had been set for the prisoners' release, but the Marlows were carrying no money at the time of their arrest, so they had not been able to make bail. Now a man named O.G. Denison walked into the jailhouse, bonded out the incarcerated brothers and took them out to his large, nearby cotton farm.

No one knows why Denison secured the release of these notorious outlaws, but it was rumored (though never proven) that he often sold stolen horses for the Marlows. Perhaps Denison felt it might be a good idea to do the boys a favor in the hope that they would not implicate him during their trial.

A lot of people in Graham also believed Denison had probably sent one of his employees to the jail to smuggle in the sawblade, but none of these suspicions were ever substantiated.

Meanwhile, back in the Indian Territory, a full troop of U.S. Cavalry had been dispatched from Fort Sill to track down Boone Marlow. They caught up with him at one of his hideouts. Although Boone was always ready for a fight, he wisely declined to singlehandedly take on an entire company of Army horse soldiers. He surrendered and was soon behind the bars of the Young County jailhouse. Twenty-four hours later, he was bailed out by O.G. Denison and enjoyed a raucous, back-slapping reunion with his brothers at Denison's farm.

Marshal Johnson and Sheriff Wallace were outraged. All of these dangerous men whom they had successfully locked up were now out on bail bonds which they could be expected to jump at any time.

Wallace decided that, if he acted quickly, he could at least put Boone back in the calaboose. Since Boone had been arrested for murder on a federal warrant, no State charges had been brought against him as yet. Wallace obtained a State warrant for horsetheft. With Deputy Tom Collier, he rode out to Denison's place.

As Wallace and Collier swung down from their

horses in front of the house, Charlie Marlow opened the door and leaned casually against the door frame. He wore no pistols; his arms were folded loosely across his chest. Wallace motioned to his deputy to go around to the back of the house. Then he said, "Where's Boone? I got a warrant for his arrest."

"Boone ain't here," Charlie grinned. "So, let me take a look at that warrant."

When the sheriff stepped onto the porch, Charlie Marlow jumped back inside, slammed the door and within a split second, a shot was fired through a crack in the wall. It struck Marion Wallace in the chest, sending him sprawling, mortally wounded, across the ground.

At the sound of the shot, Deputy Collier ran back around the corner of the farmhouse. As he knelt over the gasping, dying sheriff, a second shot blazed out of the house. The bullet grazed Collier's forehead, knocking him down. Although he was stunned, he later said he distinctly heard the back door slam a few moments later.

With blood streaming into his eyes, Collier pushed himself up from the dust, slung himself into his saddle and began the long ride back to Graham. When he reached the sheriff's office, he slumped down from his horse and blurted out his story. Wallace was dead, he told the men who gathered, but he had no idea who did the shooting. It could have been any one of the Marlows.

Marshal Johnson wasted no time in organizing a 12-man posse which thundered off into the twilight toward Denison's farm. They surrounded the house before ordering the Marlows to come out. Fortunately, there had been only one rifle in the house, and Boone had taken it with him when he had run out the back

door. The other four Marlows had no choice but to sur-
render.

"Which one of y'all killed Wallace?" Johnson
demanded. As he expected, the smirking brothers
answered with silence.

In the days that followed, this question was widely and angrily discussed by the citizens of Graham.
Sheriff Wallace, in spite of his hot temper, had been
well liked and had many friends. "Who fired that fatal
shot?" his friends wanted to know.

Deputy Collier believed it was Boone since he
had run away immediately after the shooting. Still, it
could be that Boone ran only because an arrest warrant was being served on him. Maybe Charlie Marlow
pulled the trigger and handed the rifle to Boone as he
fled. Or possibly some of the other brothers were in the
house at the time and did the shooting. The only thing
the townsfolk knew for certain was that four out of the
five suspects were currently languishing in chilly cells,
smugly confident that none of them could be proven
guilty of committing the murder. Nightly in the saloons
of Graham, a growing number of angry men gathered
to loudly and vehemently express their indignation.
Their tempers rose as the whiskey flowed.

Around midnight on the night of January 17,
1889, a prominent Graham businessman named
George Hill shouted for order in one of the noisy bar
rooms. "We all know what needs to be done," he stated
emphatically. "Since there's no tellin' which one of
them Marlows is guilty, the only way to be sure justice
is served is to kill all four of them." He downed the last
of his whiskey. "Let's get it over with."

Between 15 and 20 men wearing eye-holed cloth
sacks over their heads left the saloon and marched
toward the jail. They kicked open the door, swarmed in

and overpowered the jailer. George Hill grabbed the jailer's keys and unlocked Charlie Marlow's cell.

Earlier, Charlie had managed to unscrew a section of water pipe and hidden it under his mattress. When Hill lunged into his cell, Charlie swung the pipe in such a powerful blow that it crushed Hill's skull like a pumpkin.

In the shock and panic that followed this totally unexpected outburst, the jailer managed to recover his pistol and fire a shot into the ceiling. He ordered the now-horrified, would-be lynch mob back out of the door. He relocked Charlie's cell door.

Word of the incident was quickly sent to Marshal Johnson who went at once with four deputies to guard the jail throughout the rest of the night. In the morning, Johnson sent a telegram to the chief U.S. marshal in Dallas, informing him of the "condition of affairs" in Graham.

Marshal Cabel immediately wired back instructions for Johnson to take his prisoners under heavy guard to Weatherford, the closest railroad point. From there, they could be taken safely by train to Dallas.

Johnson conferred with U.S. Magistrate J.P. Girand, who agreed the best plan would be to announce that they would be taking the Marlows to Weatherford in the morning, but would instead move them out secretly under cover of darkness during the night. Johnson carefully selected eight men whom he thought he could trust as guards. He ordered them to assemble, fully armed, in the jailhouse at 9:30 p.m. When that time came, the four Marlows along with two other prisoners, Burkhart and Pitts, were escorted out the back door where three buggies awaited.

The prisoners were shackled in pairs: Burkhart and Pitts, George Marlow and Lep, Charlie and Alf

short-stepped their way to the middle coach. The Marlows climbed awkwardly inside while Burkhart and
Pitts hoisted themselves onto the seat beside the driver.

"Think we ought to handcuff 'em?" one of the
guards asked. Johnson, for reasons that will never be
known, replied, "Naw, leave their hands free." He and
his best friend, Deputy Sam Criswell, boarded the lead
vehicle which had been loaded with extra rifles and
several boxes of ammunition.

Two guards entered the third buggy, two more
sat down on the driver's seat while the other two
guards on horseback positioned themselves along side
the prisoners' hack. Then a little before 10 p.m., the
15-man convoy rolled quietly out of the darkened town.

The country east of Graham is rough and hilly
with plenty of dark places for ambushers to hide. But
Johnson felt confident that his party had slipped out of
town unnoticed. If trouble came, he thought, it would
come from behind when someone inevitably discovered
that the jail was empty. He believed time was on his
side; he would be far from Graham before any lynch
mob could get organized.

Therefore, he was taken totally by surprise when,
as his buggies approached the step banks of Dry
Creek, a mere mile and a half outside Graham, a group
of masked men armed with drawn pistols stepped out
into the center of the road. Their leader uttered that
classic western phrase: "Hands up!"

Johnson knew immediately he had been
betrayed. Some one, probably a member of his own
posse, had leaked his plan to the lynch mob. He had
ridden directly into a trap.

"We're here to take charge of your prisoners,"
said the voice behind the mask of the mob's leader.
"Don't try nothin' fancy, marshal. We got y'all com-

pletely surrounded." From the shadowy woods on both sides of the road Johnson heard more than a dozen rifles being cocked.

His jaw tightened. Through clenched teeth, he retorted. "These are *my* prisoners in *my* protective custody. So get the hell outta my way!"

The masked man extended his arm and aimed his pistol at Johnson's head. Instantly Johnson drew and fired, dropping the mob leader dead on the frozen ground.

At the sound of this shot, a barrage of gunfire burst from the darkness, riddling the prisoners rig with bullets and shotgun pellets. Marshal Johnson jumped down from his wagon seat, but as he hit the ground, a big, burly man charged out from behind a tree to punch him in the face, then kicked the pistol out of his hand. When Johnson grabbed for it, the assailant shot him through his outstretched hand.

Deputy Sam Criswell had also bailed out of the seat in the lead buggy and was firing with remarkable precision at the dark figures running toward him from the brush. Each time he saw a rifle shot flash in the darkness, he fired at it. It was later said that he probably knocked down at least three men before he was struck in the throat by a large calibre bullet which nearly decapitated him.

The other deputies also piled out of the third coach. The two horse-mounted lawmen had leaped down from their rearing horses, and all were now firing desperately at the mob in the bushes. They felled several but Deputy Jean Logan was hit twice, in the hip and in the thigh. He continued to shoot from the ground until he was exhausted from loss of blood.

In the prisoners' buggy, Lep and Alf were already dead. George and Charlie were wounded, and the other two prisoners were, as yet, unscathed. When the driver jumped from the rig to join in the fight, Burkhart and Pitts dropped from the seat down in between the two horses. They held onto the panicking animals' reins, hoping the horses' bodies would shield them from the incredible barrage of rifle bullets and shotgun pellets that rocked the hack.

George and Charlie, each clutching a dead brother, dove from the shattered, splintered rig and flattened themselves on the ground. Some historical accounts claim that Ed Johnson himself shouted at them: "Arm yourselves and fight for your lives!"

In any event, that's exactly what the remaining Marlows did. Crawling on their hands and knees, dragging their dead brothers by their shackled ankles, they reached the lead buggy where they grabbed rifles. Screaming like mad men, they blazed away at their attackers. They quickly dropped the closest assailants and sent the rest diving back into the timber.

Marshal Johnson at this moment was crouched by the rear wheel of the lead buggy. His useless left arm dangled at his side. He rose to his feet to better observe the battle. As he did, a man stepped out from behind a tree about 100 feet away and began shooting at him with a pistol.

Johnson was standing in the shadows. He knew it would be suicidal to run, so he turned his body sideways to make himself a narrower target. He counted the bullets as they whizzed by. When he heard the revolver click on an empty chamber, he lurched away from the road and stumbled down through the dense brush to the bank of Dry Creek, below the line of fire.

Dry-mouthed in his pain, Johnson pushed off his hat with his broken hand and dipped it into a pool of stagnant water. As he drank from his hat, he noticed a stream of water pouring out of a bullet hole in the crown. Later he would discover two bullet holes in the upturned collar of his coat... and the watch chain across his vest had been blown away.

Up on the road, the Marlows continued to shoot, reload and shoot again. Soon only one man was still firing back from behind a thick oak tree. He kept up a steady pattern of shotgun blasts in an obvious attempt to keep the Marlows pinned down while the rest of the mob escaped. The Marlows concentrated their rifle fire on the tree; within less than a minute the shotgun ceased to respond.

"Looks like I got him," Charlie grinned.

"We can argue later about who got him," George said. "Right now, let's just git outta here while the gittin's good!"

He crawled to one of the bodies for a jack-knife. Finding one, he opened the blade and said to the lifeless Lep, "Sorry I gotta do this to ya, little brother." He stabbed the knife into Lep Marlow's ankle and disjointed his foot. George tossed the knife to Charlie who made the same quick amputation on Alf.

Then, George and Charlie Marlow, their leg chains clattering behind them, stumbled off through the drifting blue haze of gunsmoke to vanish into the darkness. They made it to a farmer's barn where they used a sledge hammer and an axe to chisel off their shackles. From there they limped on to Denison's farm.

Back at the battle site, Marshal Johnson staggered up to the road to begin trudging back toward Graham. Word of the shoot-out had already reached the town. At the first burst of gunfire, a young, newly-appointed deputy, Johnnie Girand, nephew of U.S. Magistrate J.P. Girand, sprang from the deputies' coach and ran non-stop all the way back to Graham.

"There's been an ambush!" he cried out to the townspeople. "Marshal Johnson! His deputies! The prisoners! They're all dead!" Two wagons were hurriedly harnessed for a group of armed men who rumbled off toward Dry Creek. One mile from town, they found Johnson sitting on the roadside, too weak to walk.

The marshal was taken back to Graham while the second rig rolled on to pick up the wounded deputy, Jean Logan, along with Burkhart and Pitts, the latter of whom had been shot through the shin as he stood between the horses.

At daybreak, everyone returned to the scene. They found the bodies of seven members of the lynch mob, and enough bloodstains and blood trails to indicate that at least five men had been wounded before running away. To the townsfolk's dismay, several of the dead men turned out to be prominent citizens of Young County. Some had ridden more than 20 miles to take part in the attempted lynching. The identities of most of the wounded were never known, nor was the total size of the mob. All told, ten men died in this chaotic fury and at a minimum another ten were wounded.

The Dry Creek gunfight was unique in that it was fought entirely in darkness. The fight was over in just 20 minutes, but the threat of further violence remained a strong possibility. The basic causes of the shoot-out had not been resolved, since three armed Marlow brothers were still on the loose.

Two days after the battle, Marshal Johnson, with his left arm in a sling and a deputy at his side, rode in an empty wagon to Denison's farm.

George and Charlie Marlow were sitting on the porch steps, watching the wagon as it approached. Johnson eyed them closely after his driver halted the

rig. The two brothers had clumsily bandaged their
wounds with torn-up bedsheets. Their faces were pale
and their eyes dull with pain. Johnson looked down at
his own bandaged hand and said, "Don't look like we're
in shape to do much fightin' today."

Charlie chuckled. "I sure as hell ain't lookin' for
no fight."

The gunfighters stared at one another for a long,
silent moment. There seemed to be no more animosity
between these foes. Instead, they now shared a
begrudging respect for one another as if bonded by the
blood they had spilled and shed together. At last Johnson said, "I gotta admit you boys handled yourselves
right well in that little ruckus the other night."

The Marlows grinned appreciatively. Charlie
replied, "I told George yesterday that if you hadn't got
took outta the fight so early on, we'd have sent the
whole pack to hell."

"How much lead you carryin' inside ya?" Johnson
asked.

Charlie Marlow shrugged, "Couple slugs. The rest
of the bullets went right on through."

"And you, George?"

"About the same, plus a little buckshot."

"Well, I guess you both know you ain't gonna last
much longer without no doctorin'. I come out here to
offer y'all a ride back to town. Let's go see old Doc
Price."

Charlie rose unsteadily to his feet. "Damn it,
marshal, I'm gettin' tired of surrenderin' to you."

After the two brothers had eased themselves into
the bed of the wagon, Marshal Johnson looked over his
shoulder and said, "Boone's still out there somewhere.
What're we gonna do about him?"

"That ain't gonna be up to none of us, marshal,"

Charlie answered. "But you can bet on one thing: if they bring Boone in, he ain't gonna be alive."

Charlie Marlow's prediction was correct. Boone's luck was about to run out. He had gone back to the Indian Territory where he had holed up with a former girlfriend. A $1,500 reward had been offered for his arrest. The girlfriend evidently decided she would rather have the money than to have Boone back in her life.

She contacted three scruffy, second-rate bounty hunters, Martin Beavers, G.E. Harbolt and J.E. Direcksen, and offered to split the reward with them if they would kill Boone.

Beavers, Harbolt and Direcksen were clumsy amateurs in the deadly game of bounty hunting, but they were not stupid. They knew they didn't stand a chance in a face-to-face showdown with this reckless gunfighter. They also doubted they could successfully ambush him. Still, they all agreed they could use the money, and it would greatly enhance their reputations if they could bring down Boone Marlow.

They decided the least risky way of doing him in would be to poison his food before his girlfriend served it to him. So on the cold winter night of January 25, 1889, Boone Marlow ate his last plate of home-cooked pork and beans. He grew violently ill and died. The elated bounty hunters drug his body outside and fired two bullets into his chest and one through his forehead.

Six days later, the January 31 edition of the *Graham Leader* reported: "Martin Beavers, G.E. Harbolt and J.E. Direcksen brought the body of Boone Marlow into town last Monday. He was killed on Hell Creek, Comanche Nation, twenty miles east of Fort Sill, last Thursday night, by the parties who brought him here.

They did not want to kill him, but he resisted arrest and they were compelled to kill him. They turned the body over to the Sheriff and claimed the reward of $1,500 offered by our citizens for his arrest, dead or alive. The reward was promptly paid."

When the local physician, Doctor Price, examined the body, he immediately became suspicious. The bullet holes appeared to have been made after Boone was dead. An examination of the contents of Boone's stomach revealed the true cause of death.

Although nobody was sorry to see Boone Marlow in a coffin, the cowardly manner in which he had been killed offended a lot of people. This was not a deed Texas could be proud of, they felt. The three men were arrested for murder and held for trial.

At the same time, a full-scale investigation of the Dry Creek incident was under way. The U.S. Marshall's Office in Dallas was demanding that everyone involved in the ambush and the attempted storming of the jail be identified. Headquarters demanded that all details of the planning and execution of the attacks be fully disclosed.

The initial theory was that Johnson himself had been part of a diabolical conspiracy to get rid of his troublesome prisoners; that he had deliberately set up a situation in which the Marlows could be executed. Marshal Johnson, along with his deputies and U.S. Magistrate Girand were soon indicted by a federal grand jury for "acting as participants and conspirators in a mob at Dry Creek."

When the U.S. Court convened in Dallas in March, these charges were all dismissed. It was easily proven that Edward Johnson had not been part of the lynch mob. As his grandson, Edward W. "Ted" Johnson, wrote years later: "It stands to reason that if my grandfather had been in alliance with the mob, there would have been no use for so many people being killed and wounded. He could have handcuffed the prisoners and it would have been an easy matter to have gotten rid of them without bloodshed.

"I dare say the surviving Marlows owed their lives to the fact that my grandfather fired the first shot which threw the mob into a wild fury of shots and panic."

Several citizens of Graham were also charged with participating in the mob, but there was no evidence that would stand up in court, so their trials ended in acquittals.

Marshal Johnson remained certain that one of his own posse had tipped off the mob. He always suspected this Judas was Johnnie Girand since he had fled the instant the shooting started and had falsely reported that everyone in the marshall's party was already dead. Johnson would always wonder if that was the mob's original intent: to kill not only the prisoners but all the guards as well.

Two more trials were held that spring. In each case, the verdicts came as total surprises.

Beavers, Harbolt and Direcksen were tried for poisoning Boone. The defense argued that since the reward was specifically on a "dead or alive" basis, the manner in which the fugitive was slain was irrelevant. But the three hapless bounty hunters were found guilty of murder and sent to lengthy prison terms.

George and Charlie Marlow were put on trial for horsetheft, but the prosecutors presented a case so weak they could not win convictions. Although scores of horses had been "taken from the possession of their owners without the consent of their owners" in the Northern District of Texas between 1886 and 1888, it simply could not be proven which, if any, horses the Marlows had stolen. The two brothers strutted triumphantly out of the courtroom as free men.

Shortly after the trial, the Marlows left Texas and moved to Colorado, where, ironically, they were appointed deputy sheriffs by C.W. "Doc" Shores, Sheriff of Gunnison County. Said the sheriff: "They'll make good peace officers for they are not afraid of man nor devil."

The life of Edward W. Johnson was forever changed by the Dry Creek gunfight. Never again was he able to serve as a gun-totting U.S. marshal. His wound was so severe that for many months his wife, Dorothy, had to feed and dress him. She also took in laundry and gave music lessons to make ends meet during the period of his recovery.

At last, his bullet-torn hand healed into a scar-tissued claw which he was able to use reasonably well; he could hold a pen but not a gun. Eventually, he moved to California where he got a desk job with the Los Angeles Police Department.

Edward Johnson lived to be more than 70 years old. In 1933, with his old U.S. marshall's badge pinned on his suit, he was buried in a cemetery far, far away from his native Texas.

Bibliography - Chapter 12

Graham Leader. Graham, Texas. January 31, 1889.

Johnson, Edward W. *True West.* Austin, Texas. Western Publications. January-February, 1980.

Siringo, Charles A. **Riata and Spurs.** New York. Houghton Mifflin Company. 1912.

Thornton, Steve. **The West.** New York. Stagecoach

Publishing Company. November, 1973.
Walker, Wayne T. **Great West.** New York. M.F. Enterprises. August, 1973.

13

Who Killed Belle Starr?

The Bandit Queen was dead. Six Cherokees carried her pine-board coffin to the edge of the open grave they had dug not far from her home. After setting it down, they lifted off the lid.

Belle Starr looked pale but serene. She was dressed in her best black velvet riding outfit with a lacy white collar, a lot of jewelry and her fanciest riding boots. Her favorite pistol was tucked into her waistband not far from her folded hands.

The Cherokees each placed a piece of cornbread in the coffin so Belle would have food during her journey to the Afterworld. Then they walked away. More than a hundred people had gathered at Belle's home in Younger's Bend to pay their last respects to this remarkable woman. Now they filed past the coffin one by one.

There were outlaws and lawmen, friends and neighbors, journalists and curiosity seekers. Belle's son, Eddie, was there, as was her daughter, Pearl.

Pearl was accompanied by a doctor, Jesse Mooney, who had desperately tried to staunch the flow of blood during Belle's dying hour. As they looked down at the simple casket, Mooney asked, "Did she tell you anything before she died?"

"Yes," Pearl answered tearfully. "Someday I'll tell you, but not now."

Word of Belle Starr's death spread throughout the Indian Territory, on down through Texas, and out across the telegraph wires of the nation. The West's most notorious female outlaw, heroine of a dozen dime paperback books and scores of sensational tabloid feature stories, had been gunned down by an unknown assailant on February 3, 1889, two days before her forty-second birthday.

Belle Star was born Myra Belle Shirley on February 5, 1848 on a farm near Carthage, Missouri. The Shirleys' farm was located on the edge of the wilderness, 14 miles from the nearest church, school, doctor or neighbor. It was probably this isolation that caused John Shirley to sell his farm and move his family to the tiny hamlet of Carthage in 1856 where he opened a wayside inn and established himself as a tavern keeper.

Carthage was a town of only 100 inhabitants then, but it was a crossroads town, a trail station for immigrants heading west. A lot of transients passed through Carthage in those days: gold-seekers heading for California, homesteaders looking for farm land, hunters riding to the buffalo ranges, and a lot of outlaws.

Cole Younger and his brothers frequently and appreciatively drank the whiskey John Shirley served, as did the savage guerrilla fighter William Clarke Cantrill, the bushwhacker "Bloody Bill" Anderson, and the murderous Kinch West. These and many other wild

BELLE STARR. As one of Texas' most famous bandits, she lived a wild life and died a mysterious death.

and rowdy men got drunk and surly, often shooting up the saloon and each other.

Little Myra Belle literally grew up in the constant presence of outlaws. No doubt they frightened her at first, but she gradually grew to be awed by them, to admire their bravado and roughshod panache.

Carthage, situated as it is near the Missouri-Kansas border, was the scene of considerable violence beyond that of simple road agent-style outlawry. The Civil War was about to begin; the brutal Border War between Missouri Secessionists and Kansas Unionists had already started. By the time all these bloody hostilities ended, Carthage had been burned to the ground along with most of Jasper County's farmhouses and barns. The ravaged Missouri countryside was a forlorn landscape of weed-grown, abandoned fields punctuated by blackened, skeletal chimneys.

There wasn't much reason to stay on in Missouri, so John Shirley packed up his family and headed for Texas where he had heard there was undeveloped land available to those willing to work it. The Shirleys chose a 60-acre piece of land on the outskirts of Scyene, not far from Dallas. Here they built a house and barn to begin raising horses, cattle and crops.

Myra Belle was a teenager by then. Although she was far from beautiful, there was something quite distinctive about her. The cheekbones were high like those of an Indian, while her eyes were darkly expressive beneath the arches of her eyebrows. She had a sly smile. Already she was developing an independent and spirited nature as if she knew instinctively she was destined for something more than the dull life of a farmer's daughter.

One hot afternoon in the fall of 1868, John Shirley was out in his barn shucking corn when he heard someone shout "Hallo!" Looking up, he saw six dismounted riders standing at his gate. He stepped back into the shadows as he sized them up. Each man was wearing two holstered pistols, their chests were crossed with fully-loaded, canvas cartridge belts. Long barreled shotguns hung in scabbards on each of their saddles.

John hurried into the house. "Outlaws!" he shouted. "Lizzy! Myra! Grab yer rifles and cover me from the windows whilst I go out and talk to 'em." He strapped on his gun and strode out the door. The outlaw leaning on the gate pushed up the brim of his hat and said "Howdy, Mister Shirley. Remember me?"

A big grin spread across the farmer's face. "Dang me! Cole Younger! Why I thought you was still in Missouri."

"We ain't exactly welcome in Missouri no more," Cole laughed, joined by the others. "I reckon you remember my brothers. Here's John and Jim and Bob. And these fellas are friends of ours. I'd like ya to meet Frank and Jesse James."

"My pleasure," Shirley nodded. "But tell me, Cole, what was it that happened up there in Missouri?"

Cole Younger scratched his stubbled chin. "Well, little brother John here done killed hisself a man."

"Did he have it comin'?" the farmer asked.

"Shore did."

"Was it a fair fight?"

"Fair enough."

"Well then, you boys are more'n welcome in my house. C'mon inside."

The spur-jangling outlaws tromped noisily into the Shirley home. "Look who's here, Lizzy," John Shirley said. "You remember the Younger boys, don't ya? And these other two gents are... uh, I'm sorry, I forgot yer names. Frank is it? And Jesse. Well, here's our little girl, Myra Belle. She's growed up some, ain't she, Cole?"

The gleam in Cole Younger's eyes showed he had already noticed.

"I do hope you boys can stay for supper," Elizabeth Shirley said. "Won't be nothin' special, just salt pork with beans and greens, but there'll be plenty of it."

"We'd be honored to sit at yer table, ma'm," Cole replied. "And with yer permission, I'd like to be the one to say grace. But, before we accept yer hospitality, we have a favor to ask of y'all. We'd like to bunk up here for a spell. We can put up out'n the barn and we can pay for our keep. We conducted a little business on our way down here, so we got plenty of money. What d'ya say?"

"We never turned a needy soul away from our door," said John Shirley. Elizabeth nodded in agreement, and a tiny smile tugged at the corners of Myra Belle's mouth.

That night, after supper, Myra watched enthralled as these bold men leaned back in their chairs, rolled cigarettes and told boastful, outrageous stories about the dangerous lives they led. She liked the outlaws' sweaty, leathery smell and she blushed each time Cole Younger winked at her.

In the days that followed, Myra and Cole spent a lot of time together. Soon most of that time was spent in the hay loft. Within a few weeks, Myra found herself pregnant. But when she told Cole about her condition, he frowned. "I ain't cut out to be no family man," he said. "It's time I was movin' on."

"Take me with you, Cole," Myra pleaded. "I'd love to be an outlaw like you."

"Outlawin' ain't no fit life for a lady," her ex-lover

stated bluntly. With that, Cole Younger rode out of Myra Belle Shirley's life forever.

Myra bore Cole's daughter, but at age 20, she was much too restless to be a full-time mother. "Take care of my little Pearl, Mama," she said as she placed the baby in her mother's arms. "I'll come back to see her as often as I can." She then rode off to Dallas to find herself another outlaw.

And in Dallas in 1869, there were plenty of them.

At that time, this boisterous cowtown was populated by a mere 2,000 to 3,000 people, but it was as rowdy as any town south of Dodge City. There was a saloon on every corner, and even the grocery stores featured whiskey barrels on the counters with long-handled tin dippers so the customers could have a little sip while they shopped.

Scores of dusty, hard-eyed men rode into Dallas to quench their thirst and gamble away their ill-gotten loot. Myra Belle played cards with these men, drank with them, danced with them, and often slept with them. Then one night, she met a handsome, young desperado named Jim Reed. She knew at once she had found her new outlaw.

Jim Reed was a very successful bandit. Although he was never as famous as the Youngers and the Jameses, Reed pulled off a good many profitable holdups. Myra Belle was eager to join him, but when she approached Reed about it, he just chuckled. "I ain't never heard of no such thing as a girl bandit," he scoffed.

"I can shoot as straight as any man and ride faster than most," Myra asserted. "And I ain't afraid of nobody."

There must have been something in the young woman's dark, intense eyes that made Jim Reed agree.

"All right, I'll put ya to the test. Me'n my partner, calls hisself Bill Wilcox nowadays, got a big job comin' up. We could use another gunhand, but I warn ya right from the start, things could git rough. We'll talk about it in my hotel room."

When the two of them entered the room, Reed lit the lamp and spread a map on the dresser. "That's Indian Territory," Myra said.

"Creek Nation," Reed nodded. "Now, right about here along the Canadian River close to Eufalia, lives an old Creek chief named Watt Greyson.

"He's a pretty sharp old man. When the Creeks drawed up their treaty with the U.S. government a few years back, Greyson talked the government into givin' the tribe an annual payment of $34,000 in gold as a payback for the lands the Creeks had to give up.

"Me'n Bill heard that this year's payment come in just about a week ago. As ya probably know, there ain't no banks in the Indian Territory, so old Greyson's got that gold stashed somewhere until it comes time to divvy it up amongst the tribal members. All we gotta do is catch him off guard and make him tell us where it is. Then, gal, we'll ride back to Texas with more money than ya ever seen in yer life.

"And maybe the most satisfyin' thing about this heist is that we ain't really robbin' the Indians... we're robbin' the damn Yankees. Accordin' to the Creek's treaty, the U.S. government is committed to pay for any damages made by Whites on the reservation. So we take the Creeks' money, they take Uncle Sam's money, and everybody's happy, except the Yankees. So, are ya up for it?"

"I'm up for anythin'," Myra Belle answered.

"That's what I thought," grinned Jim Red as he blew out the lamp.

In the morning, before dawn while the town was still asleep, Reed, Wilcox and Myra Belle Shirley, dressed as a man, rode out of Dallas. Two dawns later, they reached Watt Greyson's simple cabin. Smoke curled from the chimney. "I hate to interrupt a man's breakfast," Reed said as he pulled his bandanna up over his nose, "but we ain't got time to be polite. Let's go!"

The three masked bandits burst through Greyson's door and quickly overpowered the aged chief as he rose from his kitchen table. As Wilcox tied the Indian's hands, Reed placed a hangman's noose tightly around his neck, then threw the other end over a rafter.

With his eyes just inches from the Indian's eyes, he said, "Now you listen to me, old man. You know what we're here for, and we ain't gonna leave without it. If you don't tell us where the money is, you won't like what we're gonna do to ya." Watt Greyson's mouth became a tight line across his wrinkled face. He refused to speak.

Reed turned to Shirley. "So you want to be an outlaw, huh? Well, let's see if ya got the stomach for it. Grab that rope and jerk that old man off the floor!"

Myra Belle hesitated only briefly. Then she pulled the rope with all her might while Reed chewed a piece of bacon from Greyson's unfinished breakfast. The old chief swung back and forth, kicking and choking. When his eyes began to glaze over, Reed ordered, "Let him down."

Greyson landed on his knees, gasping for breath. Reed warned, "We kin keep this up all mornin', old man, if that's what it takes. Why don't ya make it easy on yerself? Tell us where the gold is."

"In... cellar," Greyson blurted out. "Trapdoor... under... rug."

The outlaws threw back the rug, swung open the trap door and came out of the cellar carrying three wooden boxes of gold coins. As they stuffed the money into their saddlebags, Myra asked, "You wouldn't have really let me kill that old man, would you, Jim?"

"Hell no," Reed snorted. "He wouldn't have been no good to us dead, would he?"

After the bandits crossed back into Texas, Myra Belle assumed they would hole up somewhere for awhile, but Reed was eager to pull off another job. He knew he had a very good new partner. He had been eyeing the San Antonio-to-Austin stage route for sometime. His observations had led to the surprising and pleasant realization that only major shipments, such as payrolls or the U.S. mail, were accompanied by armed guards. The regular passenger runs went through unprotected.

"It'll be a cinch," Reed told her. "Robbin' one of them coaches'll be like takin' candy from a baby."

"But why would we want to rob a stagecoach that's not carryin' a strongbox or a mail sack or nothin?" she asked.

Reed laughed. "Just wait till ya see what them passengers carry in their pockets. Yer gonna think it's Christmas come early."

Less than a week later, on April 9, 1870, the Austin *Weekly Democratic Statesman* published the following article:

"On Tuesday evening, a most daring and outrageous robbery was committed on the passengers on the stage coming from San Antonio to this city. About sunset, when the stage was about two miles on this side of the Blanco, three men approached and, drawing their sixshooters on the driver, ordered him to stop, which he immediately did.

"The stage had on board nine passengers. As soon as the stage stopped, all the passengers were ordered to alight and seat themselves in a row. As none of them had any arms, resistance was useless, and they obeyed. After seating themselves, two of the robbers stood before them, each having a cocked sixshooter in hand, ordered them to give up their money, watches and other valuables.

"After having collected all they could from the persons of the passengers, they proceeded to cut open and rifle their trunks, taking whatever articles of value as they could get away with speedily. After this, they proceeded to cut the horses loose from the stage and rode off, leaving the bewildered and frightened passengers to proceed on their journey as best they could.

"The driver returned to the nearest stand, about three miles back and getting fresh horses proceeded on his way to this city, where they arrived about daylight Wednesday morning. No violence was offered to any of the passengers, and they all conceded that the robbers went to work like men who knew their business.

"The amount taken from the passengers was about $2,500 and four gold watches."

After two successful robberies in a row, Myra Belle Shirley was beginning to feel like a genuine, full-fledged outlaw; she definitely no longer considered herself a small-time country girl. One of the first things she did with her share of the loot was to buy a complete new wardrobe which made her one of the most uniquely styled women in the entire West.

She dressed in black velvet —tight jackets above long, flowing skirts with white chiffon waistbands, lacy collars and cuffs. On her feet were fancy riding boots. On her head she wore a wide-brimmed Stetson hat, turned up in front and graced with an ostrich plume.

With her head held high, she rode up and down the streets of Dallas in a shiny, brand-new buggy. On some occasions, she galloped through town dressed in a Buffalo Bill outfit: a beaded, fringed soft leather shirt with matching pants. For the finishing touch to each of her stunning costumes, she always wore a pearl-handled pistol, holstered high on her left hip, tilted so she could make a fast draw from the right.

Myra Belle may not have been beautiful, but she certainly had a lot of style.

When people expressed surprise at her sudden display of newly-acquired wealth, she simply smiled and said, "It's a poker winnin's. I'm on a winnin' streak."

That winning streak continued for several years. During their high times together, the audacious pair robbed many carefully selected stagecoaches, payroll wagons and U.S. mail shipments. In 1872, Jim Reed married Belle Shirley, who had by then dropped her first name. Legend has it that the two of them sat on their best horses during the ceremony... Belle in all her finery and Jim in an ill-fitting, borrowed suit.

Within a year, Belle Reed bore her second child, a son whom she named Eddie. No doubt, Belle's busy schedule didn't leave her much time to spend with her children, but she made sure they were well-cared for and given good educations.

Throughout central Texas, most law enforcement officers strongly suspected that Jim Reed was the leader of this elusive pack of thieves, but they could prove nothing. Then one night in 1874, Reed settled a dispute over a hand of cards by shooting and killing two men. Now, at last, a warrant could be issued for his arrest.

Reed hastily departed from Dallas and went into

hiding while Belle stayed on in their lodgings at the Planters' Hotel. Posses swarmed around the Texas backcountry but it was a full three months before a Collin County deputy named John T. Morris discovered Reed's hideout. Boldly, Morris kicked open the main door, catching Reed the same way Reed had caught Watt Greyson... eating breakfast. Reed instantly overturned the table to shield himself while he grabbed for his gun. Morris emptied his revolver into the table, and Jim Reed dropped dead on the other side of it.

Belle was heartbroken by her husband's death, and furious as well. Reportedly she circulated word that she was offering a substantial reward to any man who would gun down John T. Morris. Apparently the bounty went uncollected.

With Jim dead, Belle took over leadership of his gang. She now truly became The Bandit Queen. She was a natural as an outlaw leader. Her every heist was perfectly planned and timed. Each job, whether a stagecoach holdup, a train robbery or the theft of a fine horse, was plotted down to the last detail and carried out with skill and precision.

In the late 1870s, Belle moved her operation into the Indian Territory where she set up residence in three adjoining pine-slab cabins on a wooded curve of the South Canadian River, which she named "Younger's Bend." Here in the Territory she met many hard-core Indian *desperados*, one of whom was a handsome young Cherokee named Sam Starr. Sam was wild, mean and hot-headed. Belle fell head over heels in love with him and married him in 1880.

Sam and Belle Starr rode the outlaw trail together for four years before their luck ran out. On February 19, 1883, the Starrs were convicted of horse theft in Judge Parker's court in Fort Smith, Arkansas. Sam was convicted on one count, Belle on two. They were each sentenced to one year in Detroit, Michigan's House of Corrections. From this institution, Belle wrote her 15-year-old daughter a letter which began: "Dear Baby Pearl: My dear little one: it is useless to attempt to conceal my trouble from you and though you are nothing but a child, I have confidence that my darling will bear with fortitude what I now write.

"I shall be away from you for a few months, baby, and have only this consolation to offer you, that never again will I be placed in such humiliating circumstances and that in the future your tender little heart shall never more ache, or a blush be called to your cheek on your mother's account.

"Do not think of mama being shut up in a gloomy prison. It won't take the time long to glide by and as we come home, we will get you. Tell Eddie that he can go down home with us, too, and we will all have such a nice time. Stay with grandma and do the best you can till I can get back. Bye bye, sweet baby mine."

Belle spent the next year of her life weaving chair bottoms out of split cane while Sam did his time at hard labor. Upon their return to Younger's Bend, Belle did seem intent on leading a more normal life, but Sam had a score to settle before he could change his ways. He believed a fellow Cherokee outlaw, Frank West, had turned him in to the authorities on the horse stealing charge. He was fanatically determined to bring West down for his unforgivable betrayal.

Sam Starr chose his moment carefully. He waited until the Friday before Christmas when a big Indian dance was being held near the Whitefield Trading Post. Fortified with whiskey, armed with a sixshooter and accompanied by Belle, Sam attended the dance where he knew Frank West would be. A huge bonfire was burning in the center of the clearing. Sam spotted Frank squatting on his haunches near the flames.

Sam Starr walked purposefully toward his opponent with Belle walking in front of him to shadow his drawn pistol. Sam began to shout accusations and obscenities at West. When the latter grew angry enough to go for his gun, Belle jumped out of the way and Starr's pistol roared. Frank West reeled backwards, mortally wounded. But he had time enough to fire one shot into Sam Starr's chest. Both men died on the spot.

Belle grieved Sam's death deeply, but by now she probably realized that as a woman who could only love outlaws, she was not destined to keep any of them for very long.

Pearl and Eddie both came to live with their mother at Younger's Bend. That undoubtedly consoled her greatly. The three of them went riding and hunting in the deep, piney woods. At night she played piano for them. Her only criminal activities at this time were bootlegging whiskey in the Indian Territory and harboring wanted men. "I am a friend to any brave and gallant outlaw," she once told a reporter from the *Dallas News.* "I have no use for the sneaking coward class of thieves, but a good fellow on the dodge is always welcome in my home."

One such "good fellow" was a horse thief named Jim July. He was rough and rowdy enough to meet Belle's standards, so after he agreed to change his last name to Starr, she married him in 1886.

Belle Starr's wildest days were behind her now. She was still defiant and ostentatious, but she seemed content to live relatively quietly in the rustic settlement at Younger's Bend. Then the fateful day of February 3, 1889 dawned.

On that last day of her life, Belle Starr had ridden to a nearby farm to pay a visit to the wife of a
neighbor. It was late in the day when she headed
home. As she rode the narrow path that wound its way
through the dense woods, someone rose from a thick
clump of brush and fired a shotgun blast into her
back.

The splattering burst of buckshot threw Belle like
a rag doll from her saddle. Her terrified horse ran
away. Two neighbors, Mr. and Mrs. Milo Hoyt, heard
the shot and ran outdoors in time to see the gunsmoke
drift away, but could not see who fired the shot.

Back at the cabins, Pearl, too, heard the shot.
When the riderless horse came dashing in, she ran at
once to the place where her mother lay face down on
the trail. Doctor Jesse Mooney was summoned immediately, but there was nothing he could do to treat Belle's
mortal wounds. Within an hour after she was hit, she
died. And no one knew who had pulled the trigger.

Jim Starr was in Fort Smith at the time of the
shooting, but he hurried home in time for the burial.
After the grave had been filled, Starr took up his
Winchester and leveled it at a local farmer, Edgar Watson, accusing him of the murder. Starr knew Belle and
Watson had quarreled recently when she refused to
lease him a piece of land she owned. But Watson said,
"If you kill me, you will kill the wrong man. I have
never done any harm to anyone."

Watson voluntarily turned himself into the sheriff as he tried to establish his innocence. "I was at a
man named Rowe's house on Sunday when Belle
Starr came along and stopped," he told the sheriff.
"Soon afterwards, my wife came by and I left and
went home with her. Belle Starr was shot by someone
shortly after that. I have no idea who killed her, but I

know I did not and had no reason to."

Watson's wife verified his alibi and he was released. A few days later Pearl went to talk to Dr. Mooney. "Just before she died, Mama told me who shot her," she confided. "Mama said, it was Eddie."

"My God," the doctor exclaimed. "Did she see him?"

"I don't know how she could have," Pearl replied. "But in her dying mind, she was sure it was Eddie."

"But why?" Doc Mooney asked. "Why would he do such a thing?"

"A couple of weeks ago, Eddie asked Mama if he could borrow her favorite horse to ride to a dance in San Bois. Of course Mama refused 'cuz nobody rode that mare but her. Well, Eddie had been drinkin' so he took the horse anyway. He stayed out all night and when he came in at daybreak, Mama saw that lathered-up horse. She just went crazy.

"She took her ridin' crop to Eddie. Whipped him pretty bad, but she hurt his pride more'n anythin'. Eddie left home and stayed away nearly two weeks. He'd only been back a few days before Mama got shot."

"Pearl," Dr. Mooney said gently. "You've got to tell this to the sheriff."

"What good would it do?" she sobbed. "It'd be my word against Eddie's. And what if Mama was wrong?"

So there the mystery rested. Belle Starr's murder went unsolved. Then 83 years later, in 1971, a curious tale emerged.

An elderly Topeka resident named A.J. Robinson revealed a long-kept secret to a western writer, Leroy Towns. Robinson said it was his own maternal grandmother, Nana Devena, who gunned down Belle Starr —by mistake.

Devena was an Indian Territory pioneer who lived

with her family in a dog-run cabin not far from Belle's place. Apparently Nana and Belle were good friends, probably because they were both feisty women. Life in the Territory was hard; Nana was probably not at all disappointed when her husband called it quits in 1897 and moved to Ninnekah, Oklahoma, where her children and grandchildren subsequently grew up.

At Devena family reunions, Grandma Nana often told stories about those tough old days in the Territory. One night in 1911 or 1912, she was speaking about Belle, telling of how she always brought venison to their home after a hunt. She said Belle always let the kids pet her horse. Then Grandma Nana grew silent and thoughtful.

At last she said, "There's something I must tell y'all. I've held it in too long." After swearing everyone to secrecy, the old woman quietly stated, "It was I who shot Belle Starr."

After the initial shock of this confession passed, Devena went on to describe the circumstances that led to this regrettable incident. She had been feuding with a neighboring family at the time. The feud had begun a few months earlier, when Devena's boys had been given jobs hoeing cotton on a nearby farm while the neighbor's boys had not been hired. The neighbors demanded that the Devenas pull their sons out of the fields so their own sons could go to work. Indignantly, Nana Devena refused. "You'll be sorry," the neighbors promised.

In the morning, Nana found the barn door had been opened during the night, and the milk cows were on the loose. A few days later, she discovered several sacks of corn were missing from the storage crib, and fences had been cut.

Nana Devena now watched the farm closely. Late

in the afternoon of February 3, she sighted three furtive figures sneaking up to the barn. Angrily, she went out to confront them, but one of the boys knocked her down with a hoe handle. All three of them beat and kicked her viciously. She staggered back to the house, lunged through the door and took her husband's shotgun down from the wall.

Stumbling and limping, she lurched back to the barn. The boys were gone by now, but through the thick brush beyond, she saw a rider. Sure that it was one of her attackers, she thrashed through the brush to the edge of the trail.

The rider was heading west, silhouetted by the lowering sun. With her battered, swollen eyes, Devena could not see the figure clearly, but she raised the shotgun and fired it, knocking the rider from the saddle. She ran immediately back to her house and did not learn until later that her victim was her friend, Belle Starr.

Whether Nana Devena's tale is true will never be known. She died in the 1930s. Her grandson, A.J. Robinson, is also now deceased. No one can prove the guilt or innocence of any of the possible suspects in this murder mystery. Too many years have passed.

Who killed Belle Starr? In all probability, even Belle herself never knew the identity of her killer.

Bibliography - Chapter 13

Greene, A.C **Texas Sketches**. Dallas, Texas. Taylor Publishing Company. 1985.

Hardcastle, Stoney. *True West*. Austin, Texas. Western Publications. May-June, 1977.

Mooney, Charles W. *True West*. Austin, Texas. Western Publications. January-February, 1969.

Rascoe, Burton. **Belle Starr**. New York. Random
    House. 1941.
Towns, Leroy. *True West.* Austin, Texas. Western Publi-
    cations. March-April, 1971.

14

Amazing Treasures
of Padre Island

The primary coinage of Padre Island is the sand dollar. Cast ashore by the tides, these chalky, flat, white discs dot the sandy beach by the thousands. Dead and dry now, these water vascular systems known scientifically as *echinoderms* lived out their lives in the shallow ocean beds just beyond the shores of the long white island in the Gulf of Mexico.

Each sand dollar is as beautiful as a snow flake

and as delicate as a doll house tea saucer. But as exquisite as these sea-minted dollars are, they have no monetary value. They are worth nothing compared to the other coins that have lain upon these wind-swept sands, some buried and some pulled back into the blue gulf waters.

Doubloons, pieces of eight, *reales* embossed with the heraldic coats of arms of Imperial Spain, have been picked up by casual, barefooted beach-strollers and serious treasure hunters equipped with state-of-the-art metal detectors. Uncounted numbers of antique coins have been recovered from the sands and waters of Padre Island. Until recently, treasure hunters considered it a bad day if, during the course of an afternoon, they did not pick up at least a couple of "Charlies," coins bearing the likeness of Carlos V, the Sixteenth Century sovereign of Spain.

But antiquities of much greater value and historic interest have been retrieved from their ancient resting places. Encrusted cannons, primitive wheellock firearms and crossbows which had not been fired in 450 years have been wrested from the sand and sea along with gold crucifixes, precious jewels and silver statuettes of the Virgin Mary.

Padre Island is said to be the most treasure-laden strip of land in this hemisphere. The Writers' Roundtable of Corpus Christi published a book in 1950 which listed well over one hundred possible treasure sites on or near the island —an average of one lost treasure per mile on this quarter-mile wide, 120 mile long slash of white sand.

The island guards the Gulf Coast of Texas from Port Aransas to Port Isabel. For centuries it has snared ships the way a fishing net catches fish. Furious hurricane winds roar across the Gulf of Mexico, driving all seaborne vessels unfortunate enough to be trapped by the storms' inescapable wrath onto the shoals of Padre Island. There they are crushed, pounded to pieces, sunk, or thrown inland by the giant, crashing waves.

The first such recorded disaster took place in 1553 when a 20-vessel Spanish fleet set sail from the port of Veracruz, heading for Spain. More than 1,000 people were aboard the ships: soldiers, sailors and *conquistadores* with their wives, children and servants. The holds of the great galleons were filled with stacks of silver bars and chests full of gold coins from the new mint in Mexico City. Enormous wealth, plundered in the New World, was on its way to the Old World.

One of the passengers was a mystic Dominican missionary named Fray Juan Ferrer. On the night before the flotilla set sail, Ferrer had a vision. In the morning, he told the others that God had spoke to him, and that God was very angry indeed. The Spanish conquest of Mexico was an abomination in the eyes of God, who planned to severely punish all those who had destroyed his New World Eden.

Fray Ferrer implored the commanders of the fleet not to sail. When they refused, the missionary resigned himself to his fate and took his place among the other doomed voyagers.

Three ships set out ahead of the rest and reached Spain safely; the other 17 were caught by the savage ferocity of a monstrous hurricane. Only three battered vessels made it back to Veracruz. The other 14 were swept, out of control, across the gulf and were smashed to bits on the shores of Padre Island. The wreckage lined the beaches for miles, and the stunned survivors, 300 in all, wandered in shock through the broken remnants of their aristocratic dreams.

Desperately the Spaniards salvaged planks,

ropes, nails and canvass from the debris to build several barely seaworthy rafts. Upon these fragile, floating platforms they loaded all the food, tools and weapons they could carry before sailing off for the mainland. The treasures had to be left behind.

It can be assumed that not all of these makeshift rafts succeeded in making the 20-mile crossing, so additional lives were probably lost. Once ashore, the hapless castaways began an arduous trek down the coastline. Most of them were barefoot; many were nearly nude. During the first five days, they found no water except the morning dew which they licked from the leaves of plants.

The children began dying first, of course. And then the women. On the sixth day, the dwindling column of staggering refugees reached the mouth of the Rio Grande and gratefully drank from the fresh but muddy waters. Again they built crude rafts of logs, crossed the river and stumbled on.

Exhaustion and exposure were taking their toll. The Spaniards' food, what little they had retrieved and carried from the wreckage, was gone, so they subsisted on roots and leaves. The local Coahuitecan Indians, who had no love for Spaniards, picked off the stragglers with arrows from their hiding places in the foliage.

Less than half the Spaniards were still alive when they reached the Rio San Fernando. By the time they made it to Rio Soto la Marina, the group was reduced to a mere handful of wretched souls, too weak to bury their dead.

Only two men, Francisco Vasquez and Fray Marcos, survived the death march. They staggered all the way to the banks of the Rio Panuco where they were cared for by friendly Indians until they were well

JEAN LAFITTE. How much loot did this gentleman pirate bury beneath Padre Island's restless sands?

enough to continue on to Tampico, and eventually on to Veracruz.

Loss of the fleet and its precious cargo was a severe blow to the Spanish Empire since Carlos V desperately needed this now-lost wealth to help finance his war with France. He ordered Capitán Angel de Villafana to sail to Padre Island to recover as much of the treasure as possible. More than a year after the great shipwreck, Villafana landed on the stark, white shore.

During the year that had passed, other storms and savage winds had howled across the island. Padre Island is, and always will be, in a state of constant change. Overnight, a hollow in the sand can grow into a dune, or a dune can disappear and rise again somewhere else. The landscape that greeted Villafana was not at all what he expected.

The wreckage of the 14 proud ships was barely visible now; the hulks had been scattered about, shifted around, re-broken, and were disappearing into the sand or under the sea. Villafana gathered up all the treasure he could find and reluctantly sailed away, leaving the treacherous island to wait for new victims.

And there were many more over the years. From great galleons and pirate ships to contemporary shrimp boats and Coast Guard cutters, scores of vessels have fallen prey to the deadly sand bars of Padre Island. The artifacts strewn across the beaches have come to include bottles of bootleg liquor from the Prohibition Era and the pocket change of unfortunate World War II sailors.

It is also believed that several treasures were deliberately buried on the island by pirates, one of whom may have been the legendary Jean Laffite. This famous "'Gentleman Pirate," or "licensed privateer" as he preferred to call himself, raided Spanish shipping in the Gulf of Mexico for the better part of 20 years.

Laffite was one of the most colorful men of his time. With his buccaneers, he rode the seas armed with brass cannons, steel cutlasses, and letters of marque from the governments of Colombia and France authorizing his right to prey upon Spanish merchant ships. During the War of 1812, he and his crew fought gallantly on the side of the Americans in the Battle of New Orleans. He was rewarded by an authorization from the United States government to piratize English maritime commerce.

After most of his many forays, Laffite would sail his favorite ship, *The Pride*, to New Orleans where he sold his loot. In New Orleans, the swashbuckling scourge of the seas became a different man. He dressed up in a fine suit, a fancy shirt with ruffled cuffs, a silk vest and a wide-brimmed, black hat. Jean Laffite loved good wine, fine food and elegant parties. He had a beautiful wife and an even more beautiful mistress; he spent his money lavishly on both.

Laffite's primary base of operations was Galveston Island where he could hide his ships and provisions. Legend has it that he buried enormous amounts of treasure on the Texas mainland across the bay from the island, but it is also probable that he stashed part of his wealth on Padre Island.

It is known for a fact that he dug a well on the island and visited it frequently to replenish his supplies of fresh water. During these visits, it is quite possible he would bury whatever treasure he was carrying. Since the well would have to be redug each time Laffite returned, there could have been a number of well-sites scattered around the island. Near them there may be treasure holes. Or maybe not.

If Jean Laffite did hide treasure on Padre Island,

he undoubtedly drew maps, but no such maps have surfaced over the years. All searches for these alleged treasures have been based on guesswork, and none has been successful. The flamboyant pirate is probably laughing in hell.

Other Padre Island treasures have been verified as actually existing, although they remain equally elusive. One known, but unrecovered, treasure is referred to as the Lost Singer fortune.

This treasure tale begins in 1847, the year John and Johanna Singer arrived on Padre Island with the intention of restoring the old, abandoned Rancho Santa Cruz. This ranch, established in 1796 by Padre Nicolas Balli, for whom the island is named, had been one of the earliest settlements in the South Padre area. The Singers had purchased title to the land from Balli's heirs. Step by step, they put the ranch back into operation.

Their first cash crop venture was the raising of melons and cantaloupes which can grow in profusion in Padre's sandy soil. The Singers sold their bountiful harvests in Brownsville on the mainland, and used their profits to build a substantial house and a barn. However, it wasn't long before they discovered there was an even more profitable crop to be harvested from the sands of Padre Balli's island. During their walks along the seashore, the Singers and their children frequently found tarnished Spanish gold coins that the sea had casually tossed onto the beach. Soon John was spending more time beach-combing than tending vegetables.

The Singers used this additional income to purchase herds of cattle. By the mid-1850s, Rancho Santa Cruz was one of Texas' most prosperous ranches.

Over the years, John Singer maintained a steady correspondence with his brother, Merritt, who lived in

New York. Merritt Singer was an inventor. In one of his letters, he wrote that he had received patents on a new type of sewing machine, one which made a double-thread lock stitch and was operated by a foot treadle. Would John like to invest in the company he was forming? Merritt asked. John Singer was not too enthusiastic about the idea, but he could not refuse his own brother, so he sent him $500.

The Singers continued to work their ranch and raise their children. It was a very rewarding way of life until in 1861, Texas suddenly changed forever. The utterly devastating Civil War began.

In July 1861, the Texas coast was placed under naval blockade and Union troops occupied Padre Island. The Singers fled ahead of the invading Yankees after hastily burying their accumulated hoard of gold coins and silver bars. It has been estimated that the Singer fortune was close to $60,000.

Once the Singer family reached the mainland, their oldest son, Alexander, enlisted in the Confederate Army and his parents waited out the war in Brownsville. When hostilities finally ended in 1865, John and Johanna returned at last to Rancho Santa Cruz. They were shocked, through probably not surprised, at the condition of their property.

The ranch was in shambles. The Yankees had looted the house, every building was badly damaged by storms and all of the cattle had been consumed by hungry Union soldiers. Worst of all, John's treasure markers had been swept away by the gulf's malevolent winds.

The war had totally ruined the already fragile, agriculturally-based economy of Texas, so the destitute Singers knew there was no way they could ever rebuild their devastated ranch. They resigned themselves to lives of poverty until, upon their return to Brownsville, John found a long-delayed letter from Merritt waiting for him.

During the war years, the Singer brothers had been unable to stay in touch, so John was very pleased to at least receive news from Merritt. But the content of the letter absolutely astonished him.

Singer sewing machines, Merritt wrote, had become the most popular stitching machine throughout America. His company's war time contracts had netted him a fortune. John's $500 investment was now worth $150,000, and a letter of credit for the authorization of the transfer of the money to the bank in Brownsville was enclosed. Overnight, John and Johanna Singer had gone from rags to riches.

They soon moved to New Orleans where John entered into many other successful business ventures. Never again did he return to Padre Island to search for his lost treasure. It's still there, somewhere.

As the years went by, treasure hunting became much more sophisticated. By the mid-Twentieth Century, the invention of the metal detector made it possible for treasure seekers to search without digging, and four-wheel drive vehicles made the roughest terrain accessible.

On Padre Island, the searchers learned that the best time to look for artifacts was after a hurricane when remnants of long-buried ships were exposed by the frightful power of the storms. Since no one ever knew what fabulous discoveries might await them, it was very exciting to roam Padre's beaches in the aftermath of a Texas typhoon. It could also be a frustrating experience as treasure hunter Richard Clements learned in 1961.

That summer, Hurricane Carla swept the island.

Clements was one of the first on the scene after things calmed down. He was wandering the beach with a shovel over his shoulder when he spotted a bronze spike sticking out of the sand. Quickly, Clements dug it up to find that it was embedded in a rotten piece of wood.

He continued to dig and soon his shovel struck more wood. Within a couple of hours, Clements moved enough sand to reveal the tops of several heavy planks which were fastened to thick, wooden beams with bronze spikes and wood pegs. The perspiring young man leaned on his shovel, almost overwhelmed by what he had stumbled onto; he knew he was standing on top of a large section of a very old Spanish ship.

The tide was rolling in now, refilling the hole with sea water and sand. Clements marked the site with a tall piece of driftwood and drove off to talk to an old friend, "French the Beachcomber." Gene French was an avid treasure hunter who ran a somewhat ramshackle night club on the island. When Clements told him about the find, French immediately became interested.

In the morning he accompanied Clements back to the site where they found the hole completely covered with sand. The two men dug throughout the day, uncovering the planks again, and greatly enlarging the hole. Then, of course, the tide returned.

When the tide went out, it had all but erased the excavation by French and Clements. Once again their hole had nearly refilled with sand. Doggedly, the two thwarted fortune hunters shoveled out the sand again only to see frothy waves sweep it back in again.

By now, French and Clements realized it was going to take a lot more than just a couple of guys with shovels to bring forth this stubborn piece of wreckage. A barrier of some sort would have to be built to hold back the tide; heavy equipment would be needed for the digging. Neither had the kind of money that would be required to finance such a venture. They tried to find investors, but no one was willing to put up capital for such an expensive undertaking when there was no way of knowing what, if anything, was below those ancient planks and beams.

Whatever is down there has yet to be retrieved. The broken ship still lies undisturbed beneath protective sands. Padre Island won again.

One might say Padre Island always wins because it does not play fair. It invites people to come to its idyllic beaches, as tourists or as residents, without forewarning them that any beautiful day can suddenly turn into a wild, shrieking nightmare. In 1967, the third largest hurricane in Texas history roared in from the Gulf of Mexico and slammed into the coast.

Hurricane Beulah nearly demolished South Padre Island and its causeway-connected neighbor, Port Isabel. At least half of all the buildings in both communities were destroyed or badly damaged. Beach houses burst, the roofs sailing away like frisbees. Cinderblocks and bricks flew through the air like pellets from shotguns. A 75-unit trailer park in South Padre Island looked as if it had been stomped on by an insane giant.

Fortunately, Beulah took no human lives since everyone had been evacuated in time. But the hardships she created for these people were monumental and heart-rending. Still, as sometimes happens, one person's misfortune can be a golden opportunity for another. The avaricious treasure hunters of Padre Island were sure the great storm had left the beaches strewn with a fresh supply of gold coins, silver bars and possibly even treasure chests or beeswax-sealed crocks full of precious jewels.

The treasure hunters also realized that this would

be the last great treasure hunt on Padre Island. An 80-mile strip of the island had long been proposed for federal designation as a National Seashore.

This stretch of land belonged to the descendants of the Civil War hero, Captain James Dunn. People who sought treasure on the Dunn family's land were trespassing, but under certain maritime laws, the actual removal of artifacts was not illegal. According to the laws, anything what washed up from the seas onto private land was fair game for whoever found it. Now all of this was about to change.

Enabling legislation for this land's designation as a park had passed in 1962, and the Dunn Ranch was purchased with Park Service funds in 1968. After Padre Island officially became a National Seashore, federal law prohibited the collecting of historical artifacts such as flint points, antique coins or any other item more than 100 years old. The use of metal detectors was also banned.

The beachcombers of 1967 knew the free-wheeling, help-yourself-to-whatever-you-find era was coming to an end. If they did not make their fortunes in the wake of Hurricane Beulah, they never would. These highly motivated men swarmed onto Padre Island in droves, each sure he would go home rich.

Instead they found that the island and the mighty sea beyond were steadfastly determined to protect their treasures by making the hunt as miserable and dangerous as possible. The searches in the aftermath of this great hurricane turned out to be futile and frightening experiences.

The ordeal of William Mahan and Jim Koethey was typical of what all the others went through. Mahan, publisher of *Treasureworld* magazine, was a veteran treasure hunter, while Koethey, a feature writer for the

Dallas Times Herald, had often written articles about Texas' fabled buried treasures but had never searched for any of them himself.

Together, the two hopeful men made an all-night drive from Dallas to the coast. The highway into Riviera near Baffin Bay was still closed by high water, so they detoured slowly through dense fog down to Raymondville. From there to Port Mansfield, the water had receded enough for Mahan to send his T-bird splashing on through to Port Mansfield. Once there, Mahan introduced Koethey to an old pal, Jimmie Reed, who owned the local grocery store and a small but stalwart boat. "Can I take y'all to Padre?" Reed said in answer to Mahan's first question. "Sure, no problem. My boat rode out ol' Beulah like a cowboy on a bronc. She's ready to go whenever you are."

Mahan and Koethey stowed their gear on board and were soon on their way across Laguna Madre to the island. After Jimmie Reed promised to come back for them if the weather turned bad, they went ashore and set up a base camp about three miles from the jetties.

With a large piece of transparent plastic sheeting and some driftwood poles, the pair rigged up a lean-to in which they stowed their supplies and equipment before spreading out their sleeping bags.

The weather was pleasant: calm, serene and fairly warm. Mahan and Koethey spent the rest of the day leisurely exploring the immediate area with their D-Tex metal detectors. In no time, they turned up a number of Sixteenth Century coins.

As the sun set, they returned to camp in good spirits; it had been a very promising beginning. Their camp was comfortable, supper was hot and satisfying, and the coffee was strong and black. Both men were looking forward to a good night's sleep and a profitable search in the morning. But just before crawling into their sleeping bags, they noticed that the stars had disappeared and clouds were obscuring the moon.

"It'll clear off in the morning," Mahan said confidently as he stuffed himself into his bag. "Nothing to worry about."

At 3 a.m. the two snug campers were rudely awakened by the flapping of the plastic tarp and the spattering of rain against it. They dozed apprehensively until dawn. By then the rain had stopped, but the skies were still overcast and a stiff wind still blew steadily.

"Just a little squall," Mahan said as he pumped up the Coleman stove to brew coffee and fry eggs. "Today's gonna be our lucky day, Jim."

After breakfast, Koethey and Mahan headed off down the beach. They had covered a couple of miles when they noticed the sky was growing darker. Then, as Mahan described it later, "The wind suddenly hit with a roar. It seemed like the whole beach just rose up in the air and started moving. It was blowing so hard we could barely stand."

Frantically, the men staggered back toward their camp, plodding forward as if in slow motion, head-on into the howling wind. After what must have seemed like an eternity, they reached the campsite only to find it completely wrecked. The tarp was shredded into uselessness and their supplies were bounding out of sight. They watched in amazement as a roll of paper towels took off, unfurling like a white banner across the blue-black sky.

The temperature was 35 degrees, but the wind chill factor put it well below zero. Both men would surely have perished had they not been able to find their sleeping bags. But luckily, the bags had filled with sand and had not blown very far. The desperate pair hastily shook out what sand they could and disappeared inside those gritty cocoons.

The wind raged over them for the next 16 hours as they helplessly waited for the storm to end —or for the waves to rise high enough to crash over them. Neither man could sleep, so by morning they were both so cold and numb they could barely move. Mahan fumbled with a pack of cigarettes and managed to light one inside his bag after several tries.

Later he would say it was the best smoke he ever had. It seemed to revive him a little and the glowing tip gave the illusion of warmth. He ground out the butt in the two inches of sand inside his sleeping bag. Hesitating for one long moment, he then pushed himself out into the screaming wind.

He crawled on his hands and knees to Koethey's sleeping bag and shook it back and forth, shouting, "Wake up call, ol' buddy! C'mon! We gotta get the hell outta here!"

Jim Koethey struggled out of his bag to dazedly help Mahan throw what was left of their gear into their backpacks. Together they plunged into the storm heading for the jetties.

By this time, the clouds were so low and the sand so thick only the pounding surf was visible. The wind-battered, stumbling men used it as a guideline, following it as closely as they dared for they knew that the wind could throw breakers over the beach to drench them, and maybe even sweep them away. Although no giant waves hit them, the surf reached out as far as it could to soak their feet and add to their misery.

At the jetties, the hapless pair still could find no place to hide from the wind, so they huddled again in their sleeping bags. "Think Jimmie Reed will be able to get to us?" Koethey shouted. "Maybe the sea's too rough for his boat."

"If anybody can make it through this storm, it's Jimmie," Mahan yelled back. "He'll be here!"

Koethey and Mahan's situation was extremely serious. They were in grave danger of succumbing to hypothermia and might not be able to last another frigid night. Then late in the afternoon, Jimmie Reed's trusty old boat, the *Lady Luck*, appeared out of the greyness. Both men cheered in croaking voices as Reed brought his vessel's bow to within six feet of the shore. Without hesitation, they splashed through the ice-cold water, handed their packs to Jimmie and clambered on board.

"Get below into the cabin," Reed hollered. The two half-frozen survivors stumbled clumsily down into a warm, glowing room. Reed had placed three kerosene lanterns under the table, where the two men gratefully soaked up the first warmth they had felt in two days. Reed cracked the seal on a pint of Jim Beam and set it on the swaying table.

Mahan laughed. "Well, there are three Jims on this boat, but I got a feeling this Jim isn't gonna last long." He took a pull on the bottle before handing it to Koethey. Jimmie Reed turned his well-named boat around and took his very lucky passengers away from the angry shores of the long white island.

Padre Island still lures visitors from all around the country to delight them on its good days and send them scurrying away on the bad ones. With a little help from the federal government, it still guards its treasures well. How much bounty still lies under the restless sands and surging waters will never be known. Today's beachcombers can only pick up sand dollars while trying to imagine how much real wealth is buried just beneath their feet.

In this enormous state, mysteries will always abound. The night skies will forever be filled with wonders. Astonishing events will continue to occur, and star-crossed people will go on leading their extraordinary lives. Texas will always be a land of mysteries and miracles.

Bibliography - Chapter 14

Dobie, J. Frank. **Coronado's Children. Tales of Lost Mines and Buried Treasures of the Southwest.** Austin, Texas. University of Texas Press. 1930. Southwest Press. Reprint, 1958.

Freir, Paul. *Frontier Times.* Austin, Texas. Western Publications. August-September, 1974.

Green, Ford. *Frontier Times.* Austin, Texas. Western Publications. August-September, 1975.

Heard, Robert. *Frontier Times.* Austin, Texas. Western Publications. February-March, 1970.

Hutton, Kenneth. *Treasureworld.* Garland, Texas. Treasureworld Publishing Company. October-November, 1967.

Mahan, William. *Treasureworld.* Garland, Texas. Treasureworld Publishing Company. October-November, 1967.

Newcomb, W.W. *Frontier Times.* Austin, Texas. Western Publications. February-March, 1970.

Reader, Randy. Personal conversations. Corpus Christi, Texas. Padre Island National Seashore Superintendent's office. May, 1993.